The Revd Dr Keith Clements was f
Bristol Baptist College, part-time lec
Bristol and the General Secretary of tl
Churches. He is a member of the editorial board of the
Bonhoeffer Works English Edition, is the author of *Bonhoeffer
and Britain* (CTBI, 2006) and is the editor of *Dietrich Bonhoeffer:
London: 1933–1935* (Fortress Press, 2007).

The SPCK Introduction to ... series

The SPCK Introduction to

Bonhoeffer

Keith Clements

First published in Great Britain in 2010

Society for Promoting Christian Knowledge
36 Causton Street
London SW1P 4ST

British Library Cataloguing-in-Publication Data
A catalogue record for this book is available from the British Library

ISBN 978–0–281–06086–3

1 3 5 7 9 10 8 6 4 2

Typeset by Graphicraft Limited, Hong Kong
Printed in Great Britain by MPG

Produced on paper from sustainable forests

For Margaret

Contents

Acknowledgements

Any attempt at serious writing on Dietrich Bonhoeffer today must owe thanks to the worldwide community of scholars and friends who, engaging with this most stimulating figure of the twentieth century, have created a network of shared advice and mutual encouragement. For the past few years, especially, it has been a privilege to participate in the editorial work on the new English editions of the entire range of Bonhoeffer's writings, and I hope this book will encourage readers to benefit from these new resources. On this occasion I am particularly indebted to Victoria Barnett, general editor of the Dietrich Bonhoeffer Works English Edition, who has made available to me significant sections of the new translation of Bonhoeffer's prison writings before their actual publication as Volume 8 of the series. More formally, acknowledgement is made to Fortress Press for permission to cite this amount of material from that volume. Acknowledgement is also made to the editor of *Pacifica* for the use in Chapter 4 of parts of my article on Bonhoeffer and the Jewish Holocaust published in that journal in 2007. I am also of course grateful to SPCK for being invited to write the book in the first place, and in particular to Rebecca Mulhearn for her editorial advice and encouragement.

It is now 46 years since as a student at Cambridge I first heard of, and started to read, Dietrich Bonhoeffer. If in any way this book helps to introduce him to yet another generation, I shall be more than satisfied.

Abbreviations

AB	*Act and Being*, DBWE Vol. 2, ed. W. W. Floyd (1996)
B	E. Bethge, *Dietrich Bonhoeffer: A Biography*, revised edition, tr. V. Barnett (Minneapolis: Fortress Press, 2000)
BBNY	*Barcelona, Berlin, New York: 1928–1931*, DBWE Vol. 10, ed. C. J. Green (2008)
C	*Christology*, tr. J. Bowden (London: Collins, 1966)
CF	*Creation and Fall*, DBWE Vol. 3, ed. J. de Gruchy (1996)
D	*Discipleship*, DBWE Vol. 4, eds G. B. Kelly and J. Godsey (2001)
DBWE	Dietrich Bonhoeffer Works English Edition, published by Fortress Press, Minneapolis
E	*Ethics*, DBWE Vol. 6, ed. C. J. Green (2005)
L	*London: 1933–1935*, DBWE Vol. 13, ed. K. Clements (2007)
LL	*Love Letters from Cell 9: Dietrich Bonhoeffer and Maria von Wedemeyer 1943–45*, tr. J. Brownjohn (London: HarperCollins, 1994)
LPP	*Letters and Papers from Prison*, DBWE Vol. 8, ed. J. de Gruchy (2010)
LT	*Life Together* and *The Prayerbook of the Bible*, DBWE Vol. 5, ed. G. B. Kelly (1996)
NRS	*No Rusty Swords: Letters, Lectures and Notes 1928–36 from the Collected Works of Dietrich Bonhoeffer*, ed. E. Robertson (London: Collins, 1965)
SC	*Sanctorum Communio*, DBWE Vol. 1, ed. C. J. Green (1998)
SS	*Schutzstaffel* (the Nazi 'defence squadron' of special police including the Gestapo)
WCC	World Council of Churches

Date chart

	Begins lecturing at Berlin University		
1932	Lectures on creation and fall		
		1933	(30 January) Hitler comes to power
1933	Lectures on Christology (October) Begins 18-month London pastorate		German 'Church Struggle' begins
		1934	(May) Barmen Synod and Theological Declaration
1934	(August) Attends ecumenical conference, Fanø, Denmark		
1935	Returns to Germany as director of illegal seminary at Finkenwalde		
1937	Finkenwalde closed by Gestapo 'Collective pastorates' begin *Discipleship* published		
1938	*Life Together* published	1938	(November) *Kristallnacht* ('Crystal Night')
1939	June–July travels to USA and returns	1939	(September) Second World War begins

Bonhoeffer's life	*Contemporary events*
1940 Enters resistance as *Abwehr* agent	
Begins writing *Ethics*	
1941 'Operation 7'	1941 Eastward transports of Jews from Berlin begin
1942 (May) Meets with George Bell in Sweden	
1943 Becomes engaged to Maria von Wedemeyer	
(April) Arrested and placed in Tegel military prison, Berlin	
1944 (April) 'Radical' theological letters begin	
	1944 (20 July) 'Bomb plot' on Hitler fails
(October) Moved to Gestapo cellars, Berlin	
1945 Transferred to Buchenwald concentration camp	
(9 April) Executed at Flossenbürg	
	1945 (8 May) War in Europe ends

Introduction: meet the radical

What keeps gnawing at me is the question, what is Christianity, or who is Christ actually for us today? . . . We are approaching a completely religionless age; people as they are now simply cannot be religious anymore.

(*LPP* 30.04.43)[1]

How can Christ become Lord of the religionless as well? Is there such a thing as a religionless Christian? If religion is only the garb in which Christianity is clothed – and this garb has looked very different in different ages – what then is religionless Christianity?

(*LPP* 30.04.43)

The human being has learned to manage all important issues by himself, without recourse to 'working hypothesis: God.' . . . it's becoming evident that everything gets along without 'God' and does so just as well as before. As in the scientific domain, so in human affairs generally, 'God' is being pushed further and further out of our life, losing ground.

(*LPP* 08.06.43)

Striking thoughts, written by a Christian theologian in a Nazi prison cell. Whatever else, they are calling for a radical revision of how Christian faith is to be understood and expressed in the modern world. Dietrich Bonhoeffer had been imprisoned in Berlin for just over a year when, at the end of April 1944, his secret letters smuggled out to a friend began to throw out these provocative questions and ideas on the meaning of contemporary faith. In the forefront of his thinking is the 'coming

xiii

of age' of humankind: the virtually complete advance, as he sees it, over the past few centuries of human knowledge and competence to manage human affairs without recourse to 'God'. God is no longer needed as an explanation of the mysteries or 'gaps' in our understanding of the workings of nature, for those gaps are now closed or fast diminishing thanks to the physical and biological sciences. So too in all human affairs – law, politics, psychology and so on – God is no longer regarded as the supreme authority or a necessary basis for regulating human behaviour. Humanity is now mature, having outgrown the traditional support and sanctions of religion. God is edged out of the world.

Such startling affirmations – or some would say fatal concessions – by a Christian theologian would seem to amount not just to sawing off the branch on which belief and theology sit, but chopping down the whole tree as well. For is not Christianity a 'religion', that is, one of those systems of thought, activity and ritual whereby humans believe they can look beyond the world and solicit divine help and regulation of their lives? If you dismiss religion, how can you also not dismiss with it Christianity, one of its prime examples? But it is just this assumption that Bonhoeffer is questioning.

So Bonhoeffer embarks on a quest for a 'religionless Christianity', a 'worldly' reinterpretation of the biblical concepts. His effort remained unfinished, brought to an end by the much more severe conditions of his imprisonment imposed in late 1944 and culminating in his execution in April 1945. But his prison writings, for all their fragmentariness, have excited more debate and serious study than any theological writing of comparable brevity in the twentieth century. Published first in German in 1951 and in English in 1953, they both generated interest in their own right and were caught up into the vigorous 'radical' movements of Protestant theology that followed the Second World War in West Germany, the UK and the USA.

Exactly what Bonhoeffer's 'worldly' interpretation of Christianity would look like remains tantalizingly incomplete in the prison letters, and for this reason some theologians have dismissed these writings as insignificant because of their tentative and fragmentary nature. On the other hand, it is for precisely the same reason that others – and many readers at the more popular level – have found them arresting and pregnant with new possibilities for an understanding of Christian belief. It is after all not often that one is offered a glimpse into the workings of the mind of a theologian, already with a record of substantial published works, in the early stages of venturing onto new ground. Usually it is only the finished product, carefully written and revised several times over, all unintended ambiguities or misleading overstatements smoothed away, every reference to other writers and sources diligently checked, that appears for sale on the shelves – sometimes just too professionally polished to be true. In Bonhoeffer's prison writings, by contrast, we are invited to listen in on a highly learned and sophisticated mind, yet a mind still 'thinking aloud' to a trusted friend and airing questions and ideas the full significance of which he himself cannot yet discern. Therein lies the appeal to successive generations of readers since the Second World War, who instinctively feel that it is 'thinking aloud' on the fundamental questions of God, faith, right action and the Church, rather than assured declamations, that carries a ring of truth.

There is, however, another sense in which the imprisoned Bonhoeffer is a radical, namely the very reason for his imprisonment. Bonhoeffer was not only a deeply committed pastor and theologian of the 'Confessing Church', that section of German Protestants who resisted the Nazification of the Church, but had entered into the actual political conspiracy against Hitler. For a pastor to become involved in such a conspiracy constituted an almost unheard-of departure from Lutheran tradition. The sixteenth-century Reformer Martin Luther had himself distinguished 'two realms': the spiritual realm in which God rules by the word of the gospel in the life of the individual Christian and the Church; and the civic or political realm that is subject to God's rule by the law, the magistrate and the sword. Later Lutheran tradition made this distinction into a rigid dichotomy between the sacred and secular, spiritual and political realms; and whereas Luther himself was clear that *both* realms were subject to God, although in different ways, in the course of time Lutheranism bred a piety that tended to confine one's godly duty to the spiritual and churchly sphere, leaving the public and civic sphere to the unexamined governance of the secular powers and to 'political necessity'. After all, St Paul had laid down the injunction:

> Let every person be subject to the governing authorities; for there is no authority except from God, and those authorities that exist have been instituted by God. Therefore whoever resists authority resists what God has appointed, and those who resist will incur judgement.
>
> (Romans 13.1–2)

Unqualified acceptance of secular authority as divinely instituted naturally led to quietism in the civic and political realm, together with an uncritical national loyalty. The result was a combination of personal piety and political subservience. Few Protestants saw the need to question the Nazi revolution in 1933; indeed, many welcomed it and saw Hitler as God's providential gift of new leadership to a country in chaos and crisis. And even if by 1939 increasing numbers were doubtful of Hitler's intentions and competence, few would deem it the responsibility of a pastor to 'meddle in politics'. Bonhoeffer was highly unusual in his involvement in the conspiracy.

But his involvement was surprising from another angle as well. During the 1930s, if not actually a pacifist himself he had strongly defended the pacifist renunciation of violence and called for a much more literal following of Jesus' teaching in the Sermon on the Mount than traditional Lutheranism allowed. Here again, Bonhoeffer's stance was for that time radically different from that of most of his Protestant counterparts, who accepted military service as a natural duty and were proud to wear uniform. But the conspiracy in which he had become involved was one that, to be successful, would eventually involve violence: the assassination of the head of state, Adolf Hitler. Bonhoeffer personally would never be in a position to pull the trigger or place the bomb, but in putting himself in *any* way at the disposal of the conspirators he was morally an accomplice in what they were attempting, and accepted this complicity.

In departing both from Lutheran political quietism and from his earlier advocacy of non-violence, therefore, Bonhoeffer was treading an unmapped way. Moreover, even apart from the element of violence, involvement in the conspiracy necessitated actions that in 'normal' life would be thought highly dubious. It meant working under cover, pretending not only to be a loyal German but even on occasion a committed Nazi. It meant, in short, learning to lie and deceive. During the winter of 1942–3, not long before his arrest, Bonhoeffer had written in an essay of having taken part in the 'great masquerade of evil'; of having had to learn the arts of equivocation and pretence instead of being truthful and open ('After Ten Years', *LPP* Prologue). In all kinds of ways, therefore, involvement in the conspiracy and its ethical ambiguities was a spiritually perilous venture. Yet it was a venture on which Bonhoeffer felt compelled to embark in that combination of free decision and accountability that constitutes *responsibility*. In that same essay he writes on 'civil courage' as something that most Germans had still to learn, conditioned as they were to obedience to a higher 'calling'. That conditioning had left them vulnerable to its exploitation by ruthless dictatorship. In today's computerized jargon he might have said that Germans' mental default-setting was submissiveness, whereas 'civil courage can only grow out of the free responsibility of free persons' ('After Ten Years', *LPP* Prologue).

The actual charges laid against Bonhoeffer on his arrest in 1943 had been serious but probably not fatal had they come to court: repeated delays in signing up for military service, and involvement in an operation suspected (rightly) of being a ruse to enable a number of Jews to escape to Switzerland. As yet the actual conspiracy to overthrow the Nazi regime, let alone any role of Bonhoeffer's in it, was unknown to the authorities. Only after 20 July 1944, when a bomb placed by Claus von Stauffenberg exploded but failed to kill Hitler, did the regime realize what was happening, sending the Gestapo into overdrive to discover the plot's full extent and to eliminate not only those directly involved but all who were in any way consciously implicated. By the autumn Bonhoeffer had fallen under heavy suspicion. The prison correspondence largely ceased and he was moved from Tegel prison to the Gestapo cellars in central Berlin, thence to Buchenwald concentration camp and finally to the Flossenbürg execution camp, where he was hanged on 9 April 1945, barely a month before the war in Europe ended. He was 39 years old.

We have introduced ourselves to Bonhoeffer at nearly the end of his life and theological journey because it is largely his prison writings that for more than half a century have created the most immediate and widespread interest in him as a theologian. His focus on the 'coming of age' of the world, the end of 'religion' and the search for a 'religionless Christianity' have stirred interest, excitement and controversy well beyond his native Germany, not only among Protestants and not only among Christians. He is among the few theologians of the twentieth century who have prompted truly worldwide interest, from Europe to North America, from Latin America to Africa, from Australia to India, China, Korea and Japan. His statue stands with those of nine other twentieth-century martyrs above the west door of Westminster Abbey in London. It is hardly surprising that one who was radical in his theological quest and radical in his political involvement should have excited so much attention. Equally, it is no surprise that it is often asked, 'If Bonhoeffer had not died wearing the martyr's halo, would we have paid much attention to his theology, however radical?'

For theological study there is a still deeper question. Bonhoeffer died comparatively young, but nevertheless by the time of his arrest he had an impressive list of writings and publications to his name covering 16 years' work in systematic and philosophical theology, biblical exposition and ethics. His writings include a huge quantity of lectures, sermons, papers and correspondence. So it has to be asked, 'What is the relation between Bonhoeffer's prison writings and his previous theological works? Do his radical thoughts in prison represent a break with that previous work, or are they in some way a continuation and extension of it?' It is sometimes suggested that just as we would not be interested in Bonhoeffer the theologian had he not also been Bonhoeffer the resister and martyr, so we would not be interested in Bonhoeffer the *earlier* theologian had he not been the later radical writer in prison. But it then has to be asked whether Bonhoeffer himself would have become the later radical except on the basis of his earlier career of life and thought. In any case, these earlier works should be examined for their intrinsic value. So the questions for any serious student of Bonhoeffer remain: 'What *is* the relation between Bonhoeffer's earlier work and his prison theology? What light may one shed on the other?'

That means looking at the whole shape of Bonhoeffer's thought, if only in broadest brush-strokes, and seeing if certain themes can be identified that run throughout his theological career, how these themes combine, how they vary in centrality and in expression at different times and in response to changing contexts, and whether they continue into his prison theology and if so how. This requires that we take account of his life as well, for to an unusual degree his theology and his biography are intermeshed. We say of many theologians that they have to be seen 'in context'. That is especially true of Bonhoeffer, who in the course of his relatively brief career lived and worked in a succession of very contrasting contexts. So we shall look first at his life.

1

Bonhoeffer: a life in outline

Dietrich Bonhoeffer and his twin sister Sabine were born on 4 February 1906 in Breslau (present-day Polish Wroclaw), the fourth son and third daughter of Karl and Paula (née Hase) Bonhoeffer. Karl Bonhoeffer was a distinguished psychiatrist and in 1912 the family moved to Berlin on his appointment as director of the Charité Hospital. It was a comfortable and privileged home in which to grow up, permeated by the air of a long tradition of intellectual distinction, high culture and public service to be carried on by the new generation – and of intense mutual loyalty among its members. Although the children were baptized the family rarely went to church. Karl Bonhoeffer was an agnostic, but by no means actively anti-religious and indeed almost reverential in his respect for others' sincerely held beliefs. Paula, however, was devoutly Lutheran, gave Bible lessons for her children and maintained a pattern of family devotions.

Into this secure life the First World War broke in 1914. On reaching military age the three older sons enlisted in the army. One, Walter, died of wounds on the Western Front in 1918 and the family was devastated, Paula Bonhoeffer being traumatized by grief for several months. Dietrich, 12 years old at the time, carried the memory of her pain, as well as his own, all his days, and it undoubtedly helped to forge his later attitude to war. With the end of the war came the downfall of the monarchy, then revolution, followed in 1919 by the inauguration of the Weimar Republic, Germany's first real experiment with democracy, which was to last until Hitler's advent to power in 1933. The

Bonhoeffer family shared the widespread German feeling that the terms of the Versailles Treaty were unjust, particularly the imputation to Germany of 'sole guilt' for the war. But at the same time they supported the new republic, so unpopular with those conservatives who regarded the 1918 armistice as a 'stab in the back' of the army by traitorous socialists and viewed democracy as a dangerously un-German liberal experiment. Weimar, the Bonhoeffers believed, provided the best hope for the true values of the German tradition to flourish again. Despite being beset by one economic crisis after another, it was certainly to prove an astonishingly creative time for German intellectual and cultural life, and especially in the capital Berlin.

It was in these troubled yet hopeful post-war years that Dietrich passed through his teens into young adulthood. His brothers Karl-Friedrich and Klaus had decided for physics and law respectively. Dietrich was showing unusual promise as a musician, but while still a boy had astonished the family with his choice: theology, with the intention of becoming a pastor. There had been several theologians and pastors, some quite notable, on his mother's side but the Bonhoeffers had never thought of themselves as a 'clerical' family. Nevertheless, they respected Dietrich's decision, which may have been motivated partly by a wish, as the youngest son, to choose a way quite independent of his older siblings.

Becoming a theologian

Aged 17, he began his theological studies in 1923 at Tübingen in southern Germany, where he concentrated on philosophy, history of religion and biblical studies. Having completed two semesters, in time-honoured German fashion he decided to continue his studies elsewhere, in this case his 'home' university of Berlin. Before transferring, however, he opted for a quite different experience – three months in Rome. Attracted since schooldays by the history and culture of the Graeco-Roman world, he needed little encouragement to revel in the sites of classical antiquity. What he was not quite prepared for was the impact of Roman Catholicism. During Holy Week he was moved by the ardour with which people of all ages were attending confession, and still more impressed by the Good Friday and Easter liturgies in St Peter's. Above all, it was the spectacle of people of all colours, nationalities and different religious orders gathered for the festival as one believing community that impressed him. It made Protestantism seem, in his words, 'like a small sect', and he was given cause to reflect on whether his native, bourgeois German Protestantism, with its individualistic piety and lackadaisical attitude to Sunday worship, realized what *church* really meant. Before returning to Germany, with his brother Klaus he journeyed further south, to Sicily and then to Libya. Foreign travel was repeatedly to be deeply formative for Bonhoeffer, and 20 years later, in prison, he would describe Rome as 'one of my favourite places on earth'.

Bonhoeffer enrolled at Berlin University in the summer of 1924. Its theological faculty was headed by teachers like Adolf von Harnack, renowned historian of the early Church, whose erudition was matched by the huge (and international) popularity of his book, *What is Christianity?* (1900). Harnack epitomized the 'liberal Protestantism' that had come to predominate in the late nineteenth century. Its emphasis was on the study of Christianity as a historical movement, as a form of religious consciousness and an expression of moral refinement. Strictly historical study of the texts of Scripture and of the early Church would enable the original message of Jesus to be recovered, free from the dogmatic overlay of later ages. Study of the historical influence of Christianity in the world would demonstrate its moral effectiveness. Psychological study of religious awareness would show how religion, far from being an obsolete phenomenon in the age of science, played an essential part in the completion and refinement of personality. The simple gospel of Jesus was summed up in the fatherly love of God, the blessedness of the soul united to God, and the brotherhood of all mankind that would be realized by spreading the influence of this message. In an age of 'progress' and the worldwide advance of civilization – much of it under Christian influence – it had seemed to liberals like Harnack that this gospel, science and moral endeavour were all marching hand in hand. Harnack was far on in years by the time Bonhoeffer enrolled at Berlin, but his reputation remained high and Bonhoeffer gladly attended his seminar.

The most decisive theological influence on Bonhoeffer, however, came from a quarter quite outside Berlin. A revolution against liberal theology was under way, and the revolt was being led by Karl Barth (1886–1968), a Swiss Reformed theologian. As a young pastor in Switzerland during the First World War, Barth was appalled by how the most eminent academics in Germany, including many of the professors of theology (like Harnack) under whom he had studied, had hailed the Kaiser's war as a crusade for 'Christian civilization'. He decided that something was chronically wrong with a Protestantism that could only bless national egotism and cultural pride instead of, like the biblical prophets, bringing it to judgement. 'Culture-Protestantism' had identified the kingdom of God with its own idea of human progress, but that progress had simply led to the ghastly bloodletting on the Western Front. Theology was no longer *theo*logy but had become study of the all-too-human 'religious consciousness' rather than God's own self. God was being mocked. Barth went back to the nineteenth century existentialist Søren Kierkegaard, to the Reformers and above all to the Bible to rediscover the God who is 'wholly other' than the world and all things human (including, and especially, human 'religion'), who stands in *judgement* over the world in order to bestow *grace* upon it. His commentary, *The Epistle to the Romans*, the first edition of which appeared at the end of the war, had a volcanic effect on the new generation of Protestant theologians. Barth translated Paul's attack on 'the law' as a means of self-justification before God, into a polemic against the modern attention to 'religion' as a human phenomenon by which humankind aspires to godlikeness. It is not our devoutness, nor our moral insight, nor our cultural achievements, not even our theology, by which we can be saved or brought nearer to the divine. Only God's own intervention, coming down like a lightning bolt through the cross and resurrection of Christ, brings salvation, and faith is attachment to that alone: 'The power of God is not the most exalted of observable forces, nor is it either their sum or their fount. Being completely different, it is the KRISIS of all power, that by which all power is measured . . .'[1] Barth's use of the biblical Greek word *krisis*, meaning judgement, interplaying with the crisis revealed in 1914, led to his early theology and that of his followers being called the 'theology of crisis'. Barth moved to Germany in 1921 to teach at Göttingen, and by the mid-1920s was searching for a method of reconstructing theology in place of the liberalism he had demolished. This would be a theology of the Word of God, God as seen in Jesus Christ, God's self-revelation.

Bonhoeffer was gripped by Barth. Here was a theology that really took *God* seriously in all God's 'otherness' and majesty, and that called on all theology – God-talk – to face with utmost intellectual rigour the challenge of conforming itself to that Word in which God's own thought and speech found expression – the incarnate Word, Jesus Christ. It was a theology that Bonhoeffer felt worthy of his intellect and inspirational for his soul, and while he was never uncritical of Barth (whom he did not actually meet until 1931), Barth remained his most significant contemporary mentor right to the end. But less usually for an ardent new Barthian, Bonhoeffer did not abandon all that liberal theology had to say. The word of God might indeed come from beyond this world, but its impact was made in concrete human life, in historical forms of community. The human sciences of sociology, psychology and philosophy were not rendered irrelevant by theology. Rather, they had to be understood and used in the light of theology. It was with this two-edged awareness that Bonhoeffer, while sailing through his graduation examinations, chose the *Church* as the subject for his doctoral dissertation *Sanctorum Communio* (The Communion of Saints). He completed it and satisfied the examiners in 1927 at the astonishingly early age of 21. It is a study both theological and sociological. In effect, Bonhoeffer, with Barth, wished to exclaim, 'Revelation through God's word alone!' but at the same time to ask how this revelation becomes tangible in concrete, humanly accessible form. Does it come only through a series of separate events impacting upon the believing soul? Or if one says that it is in the incarnate Christ that the word becomes concrete, where and how does one find this Christ? Bonhoeffer's bold answer is to say that revelation has a kind of continuity in the community of the Church. In fact the Church is 'Christ existing as community' (*SC* 121), and by the community of the Church Bonhoeffer means a place of encounter between living persons practising the mutual forgiveness of sins. *Sanctorum Communio* was published in 1931, attracting little interest at the time. Some 25 years later Karl Barth hailed it as 'a theological miracle'.

Bonhoeffer was following the normal prescribed courses for ordination, including practical theology, but from early 1928 took a year 'out' as assistant pastor to the German congregation in Barcelona. On returning to Berlin he began working as an assistant to Professor Wilhelm Lütgert but, more importantly, also set about writing his *Habilitation* thesis, the German requirement for becoming a university teacher. The title of this was to be *Act and Being*, and it took up again the central issue of *Sanctorum Communio*, namely how revelation becomes humanly concrete. As in *Sanctorum Communio*, Christ is met – 'haveable' – in the community of the Church, which is 'Christ existing as community', because there I meet the brother or sister who is both other from me yet also for me, in forgiveness. This time, however, the treatment was less sociological and more philosophical and, as we shall see in the next chapter, was

chiefly concerned with the nature of God's 'freedom' in relation
to the world. Bonhoeffer's thesis was accepted for his *Habilitation*
in July 1930 and published the following year. All now seemed
set for an outstanding academic career, but for the moment
distant shores once more beckoned. In September 1930 he
sailed to the USA, to spend nearly a year at Union Theological
Seminary, New York, as an exchange student. This was the most
transformative of all his foreign experiences – unexpectedly
so since the sophisticated German intellectual was not certain
that America had much to teach him, least of all in theology.
Liberalism still largely reigned in America's theological schools,
and Barth was as yet scarcely heard of. Much of what Bonhoeffer
heard in the lecture halls and seminar rooms at Union did
indeed depress him, as it appeared that theology there was more
interested in bolstering the insights of psychology than expounding the word of God; more focused on behavioural science than
on revelation. But there were notable exceptions, especially the
teaching of Reinhold Niebuhr, Professor of Applied Christianity, a leader of the Christian Socialist movement and a trenchant critic of sentimental altruism in social affairs. Niebuhr
helped open Bonhoeffer's eyes to a realistic way of translat-
ing theological concerns into social realities, together with
a deeper appreciation of the social activism of the American
churches. A warm personal regard grew up between the two.
At the same time, the beginning of an acquaintance with the
British theological scene was opened up for Bonhoeffer by the
Scottish theologian John Baillie, with whom there developed
another long-standing friendship and respect.

Most of the preaching Bonhoeffer heard from New York
pulpits also seemed to convey human optimism rather than
divine grace. But he was in for another surprise. He became
friendly with a black student at Union, Frank Fisher, who
introduced him to the Abyssinian Baptist Church in Harlem.
Bonhoeffer was almost overwhelmed by the intensity of prayer,
singing and preaching here and in other black churches, and

for much of his time in New York, Abyssinian Baptist became his spiritual home even to the point of his teaching a boys' Sunday school class. 'I have heard the gospel preached in the Negro churches' (*BBNY* 315), he wrote to his family, and when he returned home a stack of gramophone records of spirituals was in his baggage. The whole urban black scene of deprivation, struggle and aspiration stirred him deeply (when eating out with Frank Fisher he would ostentatiously walk out of a café that refused to serve his black friend), and he studied in some depth both social surveys and novels by black writers.

There was yet another and perhaps even more unexpected transformation. It came through a French student at Union, Jean Lasserre. After some initial unease – for Bonhoeffer this was his first real encounter with someone from the former enemy nation – a close friendship developed. But Lasserre, a pastor in the French Reformed Church, was also a convinced pacifist, a phenomenon almost unknown to the German Lutheran who, while not militarist or rabidly nationalist, had hitherto taken the assumed line of his church that prescribed national military service as one's natural duty, since war was a regrettable but inevitable feature of a fallen world. Bonhoeffer began to look again at the Sermon on the Mount. The standard Lutheran interpretation of Jesus' commands to repay evil with good and to turn the other cheek was that these were not to be taken literally, but rather as illustrations of the perfection to which we could never attain, being sinful creatures in a sinful world, and therefore as injunctions to repentance and prayer for God's mercy. But the more he meditated on Jesus' words the more Bonhoeffer began to query such interpretation as an evasion of what Jesus himself intended: a command to be obeyed quite concretely. He began to reflect on what being a *disciple* meant, as distinct from just being a theologian. These meditations were bound up with a deeper change going on in Bonhoeffer around this time. A few years later he described to a friend how hitherto, motivated by ambition, he had 'plunged into work in a very unchristian way', but that then '[S]omething happened, something that has changed and transformed my life to the present day. For the first time I discovered the Bible ... I had often preached, I had seen a great deal of the church, spoken and preached about it – but I had not yet become a Christian' (*B* 205). He began to pray regularly.

Ecumenism, peace and confessing Christ

The Germany to which Bonhoeffer returned in the summer of 1931 was also changing – for the worse, with economic depression, rising unemployment, street fighting between Nazis and Communists and waves of attacks, often physical, on Jews, even in the universities. Almost immediately after arrival home he travelled to Bonn, where Karl Barth was now professor, for his first meeting in the flesh with his chief theological authority. In September he was travelling again, this time to Cambridge, England, as a German youth delegate to the 9th International Conference of the World Alliance for Promoting International Friendship through the Churches. The World Alliance, formed in 1914, was one of the earliest international ecumenical organizations, its name clearly stating its aim. It had promoted reconciliation between the belligerent nations after 1918, and by the early 1930s was focusing on disarmament. In some ways Bonhoeffer's acceptance of the invitation to attend was surprising. German Lutheran theologians were typically suspicious of such work, which they saw as 'Anglo-Saxon' liberal attempts to build the kingdom of God on earth by human effort, whereas that kingdom would come only by God's own initiative at 'the end'. But Bonhoeffer, post-America, believed that any church organization, however suspect theologically, that took peace seriously had itself to be taken seriously. In fact at Cambridge he was appointed one of the honorary youth secretaries for Europe. This was a milestone in his career in at least three important senses. First, it meant his entry into ecumenical peace activity. Second, while the World Alliance was a less 'official' body than some of the other ecumenical organizations, its membership being on a voluntary basis rather than made up of officially designated representatives of the churches, it was closely linked with certain of those other organizations, particularly the Universal Christian Council for Life and Work, with which it shared an office in Geneva. Indeed, the executive committees of both bodies frequently held their meetings concurrently. Bonhoeffer was thus brought into circles of the burgeoning ecumenical movement at its highest levels. And third, even in attending the Cambridge conference, let alone committing himself to serve the World Alliance thereafter, Bonhoeffer was already putting his head above the parapet as far as the rising nationalism at home was concerned. Eminent theologians like Paul Althaus and Emanuel Hirsch were already declaring that such international events were poisonous to German honour and interest.

Bonhoeffer was ordained in Berlin in November 1931. For the next two years his life was extraordinarily busy, and it demonstrated how he was capable not only of shouldering a huge burden of work but also of living several kinds of life at the same time. In the university he was a *Privatdozent* (a teacher offering lectures on a freelance basis), and his classes on the history of systematic theology, creation, sin and Christology were attracting a small but increasingly interested and loyal following of students. With some of these he began experiments in community life, with weekend retreats in a hut in the country. He became student chaplain at the Charlottenburg technical college, and took charge of a boys' confirmation class in the deprived working-class district of Wedding (choosing to live there in a flat for some time). Not least, he threw himself into his work as a youth secretary for the World Alliance. In addition to gatherings in Germany this meant committee meetings and conferences in England, France, Switzerland and Czechoslovakia. For him the main issue before the World

Alliance was theological: how faith in Jesus Christ relativizes all national and racial loyalties, and calls into being the one universal Church that must be a fellowship of peace. No less in his university lectures he was asserting that creation itself can only be understood in the light of Christ, that Jesus Christ is the *centre* of human existence and therefore the point from which all that is truly human is to be understood and lived.

The tortuous machinery of party-political democracy in the Weimar Republic was grinding to a standstill, leaving Adolf Hitler's National Socialist Party the single strongest group in the *Reichstag*, the German parliament (though not with an overall majority). Hitler came to power as Chancellor on 30 January 1933, to widespread popular acclaim, and very soon the structures of democracy were being demolished. Dietrich Bonhoeffer's own first public reaction was a radio talk he gave on 1 March, 'The Younger Generation's Altered View of the Concept of *Führer* [Leader]', a closely argued warning of the dangers of a leader who panders to the wishes of his followers, and of followers who make him their idol: 'Leaders or offices which set themselves up as gods mock God' (*B* 260). The transmission was broken off before the end of the talk, whether by censorship or accident has never been clear. The Bonhoeffer family as a whole regarded the nationalist revolutionary fervour with disgust, most notably the enforced boycott of Jewish shops already in April 1933. That same month Dietrich Bonhoeffer wrote and presented a paper for the Protestant Church authorities in Berlin on 'The Church and the Jewish Question' (*NRS* 217–25). In it he suggested three possible – and by no means mutually exclusive – lines of action by the churches: first, providing care for the victims of injustice, regardless of whether they belonged to the churches or not; second, questioning the state on the rightness of its actions; third, and if it proved necessary following the first two actions, putting 'a spoke in the wheel' of state activity. This was the first hint of Bonhoeffer contemplating some form of political resistance.

Meanwhile the churches themselves were caught up in the ferment, with calls for the Protestant Church to 'conform' to the new National Socialist order. The most strident demands were led by the so-called 'Faith Movement of German Christians' (*Deutsche Christen* – German Christians hereafter), effectively a Protestant branch of the Nazi party even to the extent of its members wearing their own uniforms akin to the Brownshirt stormtroopers. The German Christians called for the exclusion of all 'non-Aryan' (i.e. of Jewish descent) pastors from church office and the imposition of the 'leadership principle' (*Führerprinzip*) into church government: a truly German church for the German people, 'completing the work of Martin Luther'. There followed a tumultuous summer for the churches. Many Protestants thought it the hour of their destiny, for there had never truly been *one* German Evangelical (i.e. Protestant) Church as distinct from the many regional (*Land*) churches, and it seemed to them that with a new national leader uniting all Germans as never before, the moment had arrived for such a united church also. The question was what the basis of the belief and practice of the one German Evangelical Church should be. Hitler appointed a former naval chaplain, Ludwig Müller, a nonentity but a devoted Nazi, as his plenipotentiary in church affairs, with the task of bringing about the unification of Protestantism in one Reich Church. The bullying tactics of the German Christians combined with Müller's political ineptness and vanity provoked huge opposition, much of it grouped around Martin Niemöller, a former U-boat captain and now a lively preacher in Berlin. A campaign of lying, intimidation and rigged church elections led to the eventual appointment of Müller as 'Reich Bishop'. In response Niemöller formed the 'Pastors' Emergency League', which quickly had 6,000 members, a good number of whom soon found themselves in prison.

Bonhoeffer, together with a group of his students, was deeply involved in the opposition to the German Christians. For him the issue was clear: a church that allowed a racial principle – the

'Aryan clause' – to determine its membership, and that introduced political methods of dictatorship into its governance, could no longer claim to be the Evangelical Church of Germany based upon the Scriptures and the Reformation confessions. The German Christians and Müller were promulgating heresy. Bonhoeffer debated the issues in public and in pamphlets (he and a colleague narrowly escaping arrest by the Gestapo at one point), and through the summer worked on a new confession – the 'Bethel Confession' – that aimed to meet these challenges but was largely divested of its prophetic content once it reached higher church circles. But by the autumn Bonhoeffer was wearied and perplexed by the 'Church Struggle' so far, and was looking for the opportunity to reflect and recover a sense of direction. This led him, once more, abroad. He accepted an invitation to be pastor of two of the German congregations in London: the German Church in Sydenham and the St Paul's United Church in Aldgate, East London. This was his base for 18 months, from October 1933 to April 1935.

Karl Barth, who was heading the theological opposition in Germany, was furious with Bonhoeffer for going like Elijah into the wilderness, and demanded that he return to the fray in Germany 'by the next boat, or at any rate the next but one'. But Bonhoeffer's London interlude proved far from passive as far as the Church Struggle was concerned. He remained in close touch with events in Berlin and made frequent visits there. He enlisted the support of nearly all the other British-based German pastors and their congregations for the church opposition. In Germany at the end of May 1934 the 'Free Synod of Barmen' met and adopted the famous Barmen Theological Declaration that, largely written under the inspiration of Karl Barth, declared Jesus Christ to be the one Word of God to be heard, trusted and obeyed by the Church in contradistinction to all other powers, events and personalities, and thus launched the Confessing Church, that section of German Protestantism that resisted the Nazification of the Church. Bonhoeffer was not present at Barmen but was vehement in his recognition that nothing less than the Barmen Declaration would suffice to identify the true Church of Christ in Germany. Nearly all the German congregations and pastors in Britain followed his lead in identifying with the Confessing Church. Most crucially of all for the long term, he communicated to ecumenical figures in Britain the true nature of the struggle in Germany and the urgency for the ecumenical movement to take sides with the Confessing Church. Particularly vital here was the close personal friendship that developed with George Bell, Bishop of Chichester, who was president of the Universal Christian Council for Life and Work and thus the most authoritative spokesperson for the ecumenical movement at that time. Bell, both in print and in speech, declared firmly and clearly for the Confessing Church.

Bonhoeffer continued his work for the World Alliance, and it was just over halfway through his London period, in August 1934, that his ecumenical peace activity and his advocacy of the Confessing Church coincided dramatically at an ecumenical conference on the Danish island of Fanø. The council of Life and Work (see p. 10), together with the joint youth commission of the World Alliance and Life and Work, met there concurrently. For Life and Work the crucial issue was the Church Struggle in Germany and the situation of the newly formed Confessing Church. It took the firm decision to be in solidarity with the Confessing Church, and as a sign of that commitment co-opted Bonhoeffer and a leading Confessing Church pastor to the executive of Life and Work. But Bonhoeffer's own two conspicuous contributions at Fanø were, first, a paper on the need for fundamental theological principles for the World Alliance; and, second, a homily on Psalm 85.8: 'Let me hear what God the LORD will speak, for he will speak peace to his people, to his faithful.' It includes his most striking utterance on peace. Does it, he asks rhetorically, come through financial deals or rearmament? 'Through none of these, for the simple reason that in all of them peace is confused with safety. There is no way to peace along the way of safety. For peace must be dared. It is the great venture' (*L* 308f.). It concludes with an urgent challenge to call 'the one great Ecumenical Council of the Holy Church of Christ over all the world' to speak and act 'so that the peoples will rejoice because the Church of Christ in the name of Christ has taken the weapons from the hands of their sons, forbidden war, and proclaimed the peace of Christ against the raging world'.

Throughout his London time he worked tirelessly for refugees from Germany, and in it all he was an assiduous pastor and preacher to his two flocks. By the spring of 1935 it was clear that he would have to return to Germany, as the Confessing Church was setting up its own (illegal) seminaries for training ordinands and was looking to Bonhoeffer to take charge of one of them. At the same time he was nurturing a long-held wish, unfortunately never fulfilled, to travel to India, in particular to spend some time with Mahatma Gandhi – George Bell had provided an introduction – and study his methods of non-violent resistance. He was feeling increasingly disillusioned with Western Christianity's amalgam of piety and power. His mind was focusing ever more on the concrete living out of the Sermon on the Mount, and he was wondering whether more wisdom might be learned about this from the East than from the 'Christian' West – '[I]t sometimes seems to me that there's more Christianity in their "heathenism" than in the whole of our Reich Church,' he wrote to his grandmother in 1934 (*L* 152). To Erwin Sutz, a Swiss friend, he wrote about the same time of the need for 'the coming of resistance "to the point of shedding blood" for the finding of people who can suffer it through. Simply suffering is what it will be about . . .' (*L* 135). Again to Sutz, as to his brother Karl-Friedrich, he was writing of the need for a 'new monasticism' in which the Sermon on the Mount could be lived out, especially for the training of the clergy in the new context where the universities had now been discredited. Given his longstanding interest in the practice as

15

well as theory of community, the prospect of leading a seminary clearly offered him opportunity for experiment. But he was anxious to learn from others' experiences. He had already visited Methodist and Baptist colleges in the London area, and George Bell made introductions for him to visit several Anglican religious houses and theological colleges. Before leaving for Germany in April 1935, therefore, he and his friend Julius Rieger made a tour and visited the Cowley Fathers in Oxford, the Society of the Sacred Mission at Kelham and the Community of the Resurrection in Mirfield, Yorkshire. Mirfield's daily routine of prayer especially impressed him.

Costly discipleship versus cheap grace

The site eventually settled on for the illegal seminary was at Finkenwalde, a small village on the Baltic coast near Stettin (present-day Polish Szczecin). A former school served as seminary buildings. Conditions were primitive, and the routine set up by Bonhoeffer was rigorous. The first group of 23 students who arrived in the summer of 1935 soon found that as well as academic and practical theology lectures there were lengthy morning and evening prayer services and, moreover, periods of silent biblical meditation. Presently an even more surprising element was introduced in the form of mutual confession, each 'brother' being free to choose his own confessor. Before long rumours were circulating in the Confessing Church about the 'catholic' practices at Finkenwalde. Not all students welcomed the discipline, but for most it proved to be a strengthening exercise that was to prove its worth in the trials ahead. Nor was it all work and no play. There was relaxation – swimming, ball games on the beach, sunbathing on the dunes, impromptu sessions of music-making, birthday parties and the like. Bonhoeffer, scarcely older than many of the students, surprised them by his own athleticism as well as his intellectual mastery. One student who arrived that summer, a little later than the others, was Eberhard Bethge, a country pastor's son from rural Saxony. Unlike many of the first group, who were sophisticated Berliners and had already known Bonhoeffer as university teacher, Bethge at first felt rather out of place. He was surprised when Bonhoeffer paid him high compliments on his first sermon, and even more so when Bonhoeffer – who was always to be known as 'Brother Bonhoeffer' not 'Herr Direktor' – asked him to be his own confessor. The friendship that developed was to be the closest of Bonhoeffer's adult life. In due course the communal life at Finkenwalde was consolidated with the establishment of a 'House of Brethren' adjoining the seminary, a community of ordained men who among other things could serve Confessing Church congregations where the pastor was imprisoned or ill, or in other emergencies.

The years 1935–7 were extremely fraught, increasing pressure being brought upon the Confessing Church pastors and students to conform and submit to legalization by the Reich Church committees. While several of Bonhoeffer's students opted for this way in the end, others had to face ostracism or imprison-ment. Bonhoeffer and his loyal circle were dubbed fanatics for their insistence that only the Confessing Church could be recognized as the Church of Jesus Christ in Germany. Bonhoeffer also fought for that recognition by the ecumenical movement – more successfully with Life and Work than with the more doctrinally oriented Faith and Order movement. The leadership of the Confessing Church was itself uncertain and divided over such issues as an oath of allegiance to Hitler required of pastors. Yet this was also the context in which Bonhoeffer gave the lectures that led to two of his most famous books, *Disciple-ship*[2] and *Life Together*. The former, an exposition of the Sermon on the Mount, the gospel teachings on discipleship and the Pauline writings on the Church, castigates 'cheap grace', Christianity without the cross, a misuse of the Lutheran doctrine of justification 'by faith alone' to mean a Christianity without the element of concrete *obedience* to Christ. The cross, says Bonhoeffer, in some form is laid on every Christian: 'The cross is not the terrible end of a pious, happy life. Instead it stands at the beginning of communion with Jesus Christ. Whenever Christ calls us, his call leads us to death' (*D* 87). *Discipleship* was written as both diagnosis and drastic therapy for the malaise of an easy-going Protestantism that had handed the key to Hitler. *Life Together*, a much shorter and at first sight simpler book, addresses the nature of Christian community both practically and theologically.

Finkenwalde was closed by the Gestapo in 1937. Ordination training continued in a clandestine way in the remoter regions of Eastern Pomerania, in the form of 'collective pastorates' whereby students were attached to country parishes and periodically brought together for more formal classes. But police surveillance was a constant concern. In early 1938 Bonhoeffer was banned from staying in Berlin. Other pressures were mounting. Bonhoeffer's twin sister Sabine had married Gerhard Leibholz, a professor of law at Göttingen who was a baptized Christian of Jewish parentage and thus classed as 'non-Aryan'. Leibholz's teaching position was under severe threat and in September 1938 Bonhoeffer assisted the family's covert emigration to Switzerland and their reception in England, where they settled until after the Second World War.

Then, on 9 November 1938, occurred *Kristallnacht*, when in many parts of Germany Jews were terrorized en masse by Nazi gangs, some murdered and thousands arrested, property was destroyed and synagogues were burnt. Bonhoeffer was away in the backwoods of Pomerania at the time and did not learn what had happened until several days later. His anger was matched by his despair at the failure of even the Confessing Church leadership to voice a protest. In his Bible he underlined the line in Psalm 74.8, 'they burned all the meeting-places of God in the land', marking it with the date '9.11.38', and placed an exclamation mark against the next verse: 'there is no longer any prophet'. It was around this time, too, that he was learning of the existence of a political resistance, through Hans von Dohnanyi, husband of his sister Christine. Dohnanyi worked in the Ministry of Justice and, as a 'mole' within the Nazi establishment, was in contact with the growing number of high-ranking military figures already considering a putsch. But one pressure in particular was weighing on Bonhoeffer, namely the likelihood of military call-up for his age group. He could not in all conscience see himself in uniform on behalf of Hitler, but neither could he envisage making a lone protest against conscription that could implicate the whole of the Confessing Church in a stance that it did not share. Should he therefore leave Germany, for the time being at any rate? He shared this dilemma with George Bell in April 1939 while visiting England in order to strengthen the ecumenical contacts of the Confessing Church. These would be so important during the war that seemed now so imminent as well as inevitable. Reinhold Niebuhr was also in Britain at the time, and not longer after it was his good offices that seemed to provide the answer to Bonhoeffer's predicament: an invitation to visit the USA again to lecture and to serve as pastor to German refugees.

Bonhoeffer left Germany for New York early in June. Almost as soon as he arrived he felt that the land of the free was the wrong place for him to be, despite the warm welcome he received from American friends old and new. After several days of homesickness and agonizing he made his decision to return, stating his reasons to Niebuhr:

> I have made a mistake in coming to America. I must live through this difficult period of our national history with the Christian people of Germany. I will have no right to participate in the reconstruction of Christian life in Germany after the war if I do not share the trials of this time with my people . . . Christians in Germany will face the terrible alternative of either willing the defeat of their nation in order that Christian civilization may survive, or

willing the victory of their nation and thereby destroying our civilization. I know which of these alternatives I must choose, but I cannot make that choice in security.

(B 655)

Resistance and imprisonment

Bonhoeffer was back home at the end of July. Little more than a month later Germany was at war. For much of the first year of war the clandestine ordination courses continued in Eastern Pomerania, until even these were closed down by the Gestapo. Bonhoeffer was forbidden to speak in public and had to report regularly to the police. Not that he was now in forced inactivity, for the Confessing Church seconded him for 'theological work', which meant in effect the book he had so long wanted to write, *Ethics*. Meanwhile, in the summer of 1940 another course opened up, that of active involvement in the political resistance of which he had been aware for at least two years through Hans von Dohnanyi. There were in fact several 'resistance' circles and movements of opposition to the regime. The one that was to culminate in the July Plot of 1944 involved both the army and highly placed civilians, and the co-ordination between the two wings took place largely in Dohnanyi's office in the Ministry of Justice. On the military side the centre was in the *Abwehr*, the counter-intelligence agency directed by Admiral Walter-Wilhelm Canaris. The official and ostensible function of the *Abwehr* was to gather intelligence about the political scene abroad and among Germany's enemies in particular. Under Canaris, however, it was secretly aiming to make contacts with those abroad who might support an overthrow of Hitler. In the summer of 1940 Hans von Dohnanyi had serious discussions with Bonhoeffer about the possibility of his being taken on by the *Abwehr* as one of its agents. The fact of his having many ecumenical contacts abroad would serve well as an official justification for his service (intelligence services had after all to use people of many different backgrounds and even dubious political credentials), but more to the point it would serve the even more clandestine task of communicating information about the resistance to circles abroad who could be vital to its success.

Bonhoeffer agreed despite all the moral risks involved in conspiracy, even one that would eventually require an attempt at the assassination of Hitler. At the same time, being taken on as an official agent of the *Abwehr* would for a while at least provide exemption from the military call-up, the threat of which loomed continually. So Bonhoeffer was taken on as an unpaid agent attached to the *Abwehr* Munich office. Other members of the Bonhoeffer family circle who became involved in the conspiracy were his brother Klaus, and brother-in-law Rüdiger Schleicher, husband of his sister Ursula.

Bonhoeffer from now on was living the shadowy life of a double agent, outwardly a loyal German serving his country, inwardly working against its leadership for the sake of its eventual reconstruction. All the time, meanwhile, he was writing his *Ethics* (for some of the time in the seclusion of the Benedictine monastery at Ettal in Bavaria), wrestling with the issues of what constitutes responsibility, how one cannot at times avoid guilt in responsible action, and what it means to 'tell the truth', all in a context where the traditional rules and guidelines had become useless. It was also at one level a lonely life, since even within the Confessing Church only his closest intimates, notably Eberhard Bethge, knew what he was actually involved in. It was the family circle, itself so bound up with the conspiracy, that now became the most significant 'community' for him. An additional element, however, entered during these war years. An earlier relationship with a fellow Berlin student, Elisabeth Zinn, had not survived the demands of the Church Struggle in the Finkenwalde period, during which Bonhoeffer himself was counselling his students that now was not the time to think of marriage. Ironically, it was during these even more perilous war years that he now fell in love with Maria von Wedemeyer, almost half his age and whose confirmation class he had conducted. She was the granddaughter of Ruth von Kleist-Retzow, an aristocratic widow who had been a firm friend of the Finkenwalde seminary and who, after its closure, continued to entertain Bonhoeffer and his colleagues on her family estate at Klein-Krössin in Pomerania. The couple's engagement took place in early 1943 but was not made public until after Bonhoeffer's arrest.

In October 1941 the first mass deportations of Jews eastward from Berlin took place. Hans von Dohnanyi enlisted Bonhoeffer in an *Abwehr* operation, code-named Operation 7, that enabled a number of Jews, ostensibly recruited as *Abwehr* agents, to travel to Switzerland with the officially stated purpose of gaining intelligence about enemy thinking and planning, but in fact in order to escape from Germany for good. Bonhoeffer put at their disposal his ecumenical contacts in the neutral country to facilitate their reception. But most of Bonhoeffer's work within the *Abwehr* involved his own travels. In all he made six foreign trips during 1941–2, to Norway, Switzerland, Italy and Sweden. The three visits to Switzerland were particularly important in sharing and receiving information in the secretariat of the World Council of Churches in Geneva, and it was during his third such visit in May 1942 that he learned that Bishop George Bell was at that moment in neutral Sweden. Hastening back to Berlin he obtained a special *Abwehr* travel permit and was able to find Bell at Sigtuna just outside Stockholm. Bonhoeffer briefed Bell in detail on the resistance, the plans for an overthrow of the regime and the installation of a new, non-Nazi government. The leaders of the resistance were anxious to know if Britain and the other allies would negotiate with such a government. On his return to London Bell met with Anthony Eden, the British foreign secretary, with this information and the question. But no positive answer came and the resistance had to continue in the dark.

Bonhoeffer was arrested at his parents' home in Berlin on 5 April 1943. He was placed in the Tegel military prison under suspicion of using his *Abwehr* service as a pretext for evading conscription, and there were questions also about Operation 7. The prison experience was undoubtedly a severe psychological trial for Bonhoeffer though not, for the first year or so, a particularly dangerous one (apart from the intensive RAF bombing of Berlin at the end of 1943). He was able to have visits from his family, friends and fiancée, receive gifts of food, clothes and books, and to write a certain number of letters. He was anxious for the legal case against him to be resolved, but the investigations proved tediously long and were indefinitely delayed when his papers were lost in the air raids. Secret messages about his and other family members' interrogations (Hans von Dohnanyi had also been arrested) were exchanged using a system of minute dots pencilled under letters in books sent in and returned. He established a routine of reading and writing as well as maintaining his discipline of Bible reading, meditation and prayer, and he became something of a hero among fellow-prisoners and warders alike for his calmness even during the worst air raids and his readiness to help those injured and troubled in any way. The secret correspondence with Eberhard Bethge, smuggled out by a sympathetic warder, began in the autumn of 1943. As well as letters there were attempts at writing novels, a play and, in a new and remarkable venture for Bonhoeffer, a number of poems.

The 'radical' themes in the letters to Bethge appear from the end of April 1944. Bethge had enlisted in the army after Bonhoeffer's arrest (uniform being the best camouflage for opponents of the regime), and by now was serving in Italy. He had also married Bonhoeffer's niece Renate Schleicher, and their son, named Dietrich after his great-uncle, was born in February 1944. For his baptism in May 1944 Bonhoeffer sent from prison a sermon that, as well as containing many appropriate family references, is also a vehicle for some of his new ideas on the future of the Church and should therefore be considered as belonging to his radical writings.

'The end, for me the beginning'

The failed attempt of the bomb plot against Hitler on 20 July 1944 drastically increased the danger for Bonhoeffer and anyone else already under suspicion. In late September the Gestapo found files in the *Abwehr* bunker at Zossen, just outside Berlin, that directly implicated Dohnanyi and his circle. A plan for Bonhoeffer to escape from Tegel was hatched but abandoned for fear of reprisals against the family. Shortly afterwards he was transferred to the Gestapo cellars in the centre of Berlin. His interrogations were verbally repellent though apparently without the use of physical torture, and it was from there that he wrote the new-year poem for Maria von Wedemeyer, 'By gracious powers, so wonderfully protected', which has found its way into many hymnbooks. Early in 1945 he was transferred south to Buchenwald concentration camp. Just after Easter, the US army closing in from the west, he was transported with other prisoners into Bavaria. Two British officers in the party, Hugh Falconer and Payne Best, later wrote vivid recollections of 'Pastor Bonhoeffer', his faith, serenity, cheerfulness and kindliness: 'He was one of the very few men I have ever met to whom his God was real and ever close to him,' said Best.[3] In a schoolroom in the village of Schön-berg, on the morning of Low Sunday, Bonhoeffer conducted a short service for the prisoners. As it was ending, two Gestapo in plain clothes came in and demanded Bonhoeffer go with them. He had time to tell Best, 'This is the end, for me the beginning', and asked him to convey greetings and brotherly solidarity to George Bell if ever he had the chance to do so.

Bonhoeffer was taken by road to Flossenbürg, the notorious execution camp near the Czech border. There, he and six other remaining conspirators, including Admiral Canaris, each faced a summary SS court martial and the next morning, 9 April, were hanged, probably with prolonged barbarity. By then or soon after, in Berlin, Hans von Dohnanyi, Klaus Bonhoeffer and Rüdiger Schleicher had also died under Hitler's final revenge.

2

Persistent themes: Christ, sociality, this-worldliness and 'one realm'

Dietrich Bonhoeffer's theology developed through several phases marked by distinct interests and different emphases. But equally, certain key themes run throughout his thought. These themes form a pattern that varies from one phase to another, from one context and its challenges to another, as one issue becomes more dominant relative to the others or is modified in the light of the others. But rarely is any one of these themes completely absent. In this chapter we shall look at four such themes that run from his postgraduate dissertations, *Sanctorum Communio* and *Act and Being*, right through to his *Ethics* in the context of the wartime resistance. We shall then be in a position to look again at the 'radical' prison letters and to ask whether and to what extent those letters mark a real break with his earlier thought, or yet another variation of the earlier pattern.

The four themes are: God in Christ; the sociality of human existence; this-worldliness; and thinking in one realm.

God in Christ

Karl Barth throughout his days kept above his desk a reproduction of one of the most famous paintings of the crucifixion: the Isenheim altarpiece painted by Matthias Grünewald in the early sixteenth century. Against a forbiddingly dark background the light falls on the dying Jesus depicted with almost too cruel realism. Close by stands John the Baptist, his long, bony finger pointing to the cross, with his words, 'He must grow greater, I must grow less.' This for Barth provided the model of *Christo-centricity*, theology that is centred on Christ as the revelation of God. God is transcendent, wholly other than the world, hidden except at *this* point, to which John points.

Barth's Christocentricity became fundamental for Bonhoeffer when he first read Barth in the winter of 1924–5, and it remained so throughout his life. Bonhoeffer always spoke in the Barthian language of God's transcendence and Christocentric self-revelation. He did so, however, in an accent clearly his own. If we can imagine both Barth and Bonhoeffer standing before Grünewald's picture, Barth, following the line of the Baptist's finger, would be saying of the one on the cross, 'There, and there alone!' Bonhoeffer, however, would be pointing out that there are three other figures in the scene: a distraught but ador-ing Mary Magdalene at the foot of the cross, and Jesus' mother and the Beloved Disciple embracing in mutual consolation, and he would be saying, 'Yes, but Jesus is not alone; he's in the midst of people!' Barth's 'Only here!' is matched by Bonhoeffer's 'Here God *really is*, on earth, in history, and among real people.' This is a vital element in the young Bonhoeffer's two dissertations, *Sanctorum Communio* and *Act and Being*. In the first, Bonhoeffer wants to make God's self-revelation in Jesus Christ concrete, real, 'haveable': not just an uttered word, speech in the air, still less an abstract doctrine, but rather something more continuous, earthed and experienced in the community of the Church. So too in *Act and Being*, only here the dialogue is less with sociology and more with contemporary theologies (especially Barth) and philosophies – particularly, as far as the latter were concerned, with Martin Heidegger, the existentialist whose *Being and Time* had just appeared in 1927. Bonhoeffer's quarrel with the phil-osophers was that regardless of whether they were 'idealists' (viewing human reason as itself an expression of the universal reason and so giving us the possibility of knowing ultimate truth without looking outside ourselves) or 'existentialists' (making the truth a matter of our own decision), truth for the philosophers still lay enclosed within the knowing person ('the subject'). But according to the biblical and Reformation faith, truth and salvation lie *outside* of our selves, in the Christ who is beyond ourselves (*extra nos*) yet also 'for us' (*pro nobis*) in his grace. These were Martin Luther's terms, and Bonhoeffer further used Luther's description of original sin, 'the heart turned in on itself' (*cor incurvum in se*), as a diagnosis not only of the sickness of the human heart but also of a fatal weakness in contemporary philosophy. As against these philosophies and their religious forms Bonhoeffer sided with Barth: God is 'other' than us and so therefore is God's truth. But while, with Barth, Bonhoeffer stood for the majesty and freedom of God in distinction from the world, he was not satisfied with Barth's 'wholly other' God who seemed to be in sheer opposition to the world, a God whose godness was a freedom *from* the world. Was this truly biblical? Once again Bonhoeffer turns to Luther's Christ, who is both *extra nos* yet *pro nobis*, apart from us yet utterly *for* us in his grace, and he recasts the notion of God's 'freedom':

> It is a question of the freedom of God, which finds its strongest evidence precisely in that God freely chose to be bound to historical human beings and to be placed at the disposal of human beings. God is free not from human beings but for them. Christ is the word of God's freedom. God *is* present . . . 'haveable', graspable in the Word within the church.
>
> (*AB* 90f.)

So Bonhoeffer follows Barth in saying, 'Christ alone', but wants also to ask, 'How and where do we meet this God-revealing Christ?' Christ the Word of God cannot just be an abstract formula, but is a person met concretely and experienced through the medium of a human community ('the Church') living by the forgiveness of sins. This leaves us itching to ask Bonhoeffer: 'But isn't that making Christ a bit *too* human? How can he be met in the form of a human community and yet worshipped as God?' Bonhoeffer's reply would be, 'That's exactly what we have to look at again in the understanding of the person of Christ (Christology). Come to my lectures in Berlin 1933!'

These Christology lectures are in fact only available to us as reconstructed from students' notes – and incomplete at that. Nor can it be pretended that they are easy to understand. But it is in them that we find the nub of the theology on which hangs so much else that he wrote. On one level they are an exposition of the traditional credal statements, of Jesus being truly divine and truly human, and of being one person in two natures, divine and human. But if we come expecting to find some 'explanation' of 'how' Jesus can be both human and divine we are in for a rude shock, for Bonhoeffer brusquely dismisses all 'How?' questions. They belong to the area where human reason operates, and the claim that Jesus Christ is the Word of God means, if it means anything at all, that this area has met its limit in encounter with the eternal. The 'How?' question envisages Jesus as a kind of chemical compound, part humanity and part divinity, and looks for a formula by which these two can be held together. Not 'How?' but 'Who?' is the real question. 'One does not first look at a human nature and then beyond it to a divine nature, but one has to do with the one man Jesus Christ, who is fully God' (*C* 108). What Bonhoeffer is above all attacking is the notion that Jesus' 'special' quality as divine-and-human can first be established and explained, and that *then* we can go on to talk about his love, his grace, his saving work for humanity. Instead, according to Bonhoeffer, Christ's being 'for us' is not a fact about him that is 'additional' to his being 'true God and true man'. Christ's 'being for us' is the very essence of his divinity and humanity and their unity. Jesus is 'the incarnate one, the unveiled image of God' (*C* 109). It is precisely in his humanity that Jesus glorifies and reveals God.

Not only so, but he is also the humiliated one, disowned, rejected, crucified. Far from this contradicting his divinity, Jesus as humanly humiliated remains wholly God: 'We say of the humiliated one, "This is God". He makes none of his divine properties manifest in his death. On the contrary, we see a man doubting God as he dies. But of this man we say, "This is God"' (*C* 110). Here is where is seen, hidden except to faith, the divine freedom, free to be *pro nobis*, for us, in the extremity of human life and death. No less in his resurrection and exaltation he remains 'for us', proclaimed as available in word and sacrament. We find this Christology of Jesus 'for us' underpinning all Bonhoeffer's mature theology.

In keeping with his insistence on the concrete, the real here-and-nowness of Jesus the incarnate Word, Bonhoeffer's Christocentricity had vital practical application. Especially, it stamped his efforts during 1931–3 to counter the rising impulses of nationalist theology. Both by the Nazi 'German Christians' and by certain more sophisticated theologians, much was being made of 'a theology of creation' in order to boost the claims of race and nationhood as divinely instituted 'orders'. 'Orders of creation' was a traditional Protestant concept, recognizing that certain features of human existence, such as marriage, family, work and so on, were divinely ordained for human welfare. The nationalist theology, however, was elevating 'orders of creation' to unprecedented significance equal to that of redemption, and moreover making race, people (*Volk*) and nation *the* most significant orders, which had to be 'preserved in their purity' at all costs. It was particularly at meetings of the World Alliance, both in Germany and elsewhere, that Bonhoeffer combated such ideas that in his view denied Jesus Christ and the gospel as the key theological vantage point for viewing all human existence. In effect, to make nation and race 'orders of creation' was to sanctify racism and provide a theological justification for war. In the light of Christ, Bonhoeffer argued, race and nation were not 'orders of creation' but provisional structures that God providentially allows as 'orders of *preservation*' that may in fact be *broken down* if they prove to be obstructing the gospel. 'The Church hears the commandment only from Christ, not from any fixed law or from any eternal order' (*NRS* 167). This Christocentric approach that Bonhoeffer pressed within the World Alliance was of a piece with the university lectures on creation that he was giving at the same time in Berlin. Here, he treats creation and sin by expounding the early chapters of Genesis, but even when dealing with the Old Testament (which in itself, in an increasingly anti-Semitic climate, was provocative!), he insisted on reading the text in the light of Jesus Christ as the key to its 'theological' understanding. 'Where Holy Scripture, upon which the Church of Christ stands, speaks of creation, of the beginning, what else can it say other than that it is only from Christ that we can know what the beginning is?' (*CF* 22). Set as we are as sinful people in a fallen world, the only way we can really glimpse the original paradise is by looking to the one who has restored creation to its divine purpose.

This was the basic theological objection to that kind of Germanic Protestantism that, independently of the revelation in Christ, claimed to be able to read the divine purpose straight off from the world as it is, from history as it appeared to be developing, from excitements surging in the national life and its apparent renewal under Hitler. Hence the opening thesis of the Barmen Theological Declaration of May 1934, largely drafted by Karl Barth, on which was founded the Confessing Church:

> Jesus Christ, as he is testified to us in Holy Scripture, is the one Word of God, which we are to hear, which we are to trust and obey in life and in death.
>
> We repudiate the false teaching that the Church can and must recognize yet other happenings and powers, personalities and truths, alongside this one Word of God, as a source of her preaching.[1]

For Bonhoeffer, the time called for a clear distinction between obedience to the gospel of Christ and the Germanic paganism of blood, race and soil being promoted by the German Christians, and being tolerated by the Reich Church. Throughout the Church Struggle Bonhoeffer was uncompromising: only those who adhered to the Barmen Declaration, that is, the Confessing Church, could rightly claim to be the German Evangelical Church because only that Church was clearly confessing *Christ* as distinct from German national and religious feeling. 'So the call to discipleship is a commitment solely to the person of Jesus Christ, a breaking through of all legalisms by the grace of him who calls' (*D* 59), writes Bonhoeffer in *Discipleship*. That book was a concrete spelling out of what the Barmen Declaration meant for individual Christians and communities. Ten years after Bonhoeffer's death, Karl Barth confessed when expounding the subject of sanctification in his mighty *Church Dogmatics*, that he was tempted simply to insert the opening chapters of *Discipleship* as an extended quotation!

The sociality of human existence

'The Church is Christ existing as community' (*SC* 121). In fact the German philosophical and theological scene of the 1920s was alive with 'personalist' and 'relational' understandings of human existence, which stressed that to be human means to live in encounter and relationship with others rather than as either an isolated individual or as part of an impersonal 'mass'. Bonhoeffer's doctoral supervisor, the systematic theologian Reinhold Seeberg, was himself a powerful advocate of the 'sociality' of human existence. The young Bonhoeffer drew selectively and critically upon much of this contemporary thought, but above all sought to ground it Christologically in the Christ who is apart from us, yet for us. As we have seen, in *Act and Being* and the Christology lectures, this being-for-us is the essence of Christ as God incarnate, not some addition to it. From now on, for Bonhoeffer sociality is measured in Christological terms, and Christ is seen in relational, 'being-for' terms. Christ's 'being-for-us' is thus the basis of all human sociality.

Looking further at a section of the Christology lectures, we see in a condensed but remarkable passage how Bonhoeffer uses his 'Christ for me' concept to recast, in effect, the traditional language of Christ as 'judge' and 'saviour', and of human beings as sinful and in need of grace:

> [Jesus Christ] stands in my place, where I should stand and cannot. He stands on the boundary of existence, beyond my existence, but still for me. This expresses the fact that I am separated from the 'I' that I should be by a boundary which I am unable to cross. This boundary lies between me and myself, between the old 'I' and the new 'I'. I am judged in my encounter with this boundary. At this place I cannot stand alone. Here Christ stands, in the centre, between me and myself, between the old existence and the new. So Christ is at the same time my own boundary and my rediscovered centre, the centre lying between 'I' and 'I' and between 'I' and God. The boundary can only be known as a boundary from beyond the boundary. In Christ man knows it and thus at the same time finds his new centre.
>
> (*C* 61f.)

On this basis, Bonhoeffer goes on to speak of Jesus Christ, the one who is 'for me', as the one whose very nature is to be at the 'centre' of human existence, of history and of nature. To paraphrase Bonhoeffer, Jesus in his nature as 'being-for-us' both reveals and enables truly human existence. So it is no surprise, either, that in his exposition of the creation of humankind we find Bonhoeffer speaking of 'the image of God' in humanity as reflecting God's own freedom, which, as set out in *Act and Being*, is the freedom of the grace by which God binds Godself to human beings. 'For in the language of the Bible freedom is not something that people have for themselves but something they have for others . . . freedom . . . is a relation and nothing else' (*CF* 62). 'Only in relationship with the other am I free.' God creates humankind male and female, signifying that to be human is not to be alone but in duality, and it is in this mutual dependence that human creatureliness consists.

From this very tight theological centre of the fusion of Christ and sociality there sounds a chord that resonates in so much else of Bonhoeffer's thought. It is no accident that at the same time as lecturing on Christology, creation and human relationality, he was actively promoting the ecumenical peace cause through the World Alliance (see Chapter 2). Thereby he was challenging the ecumenical movement really to live up to its calling and to embody the universal fellowship of Christ that transcends all national and racial boundaries, whose members are bound together by the word of Christ more closely than by all human ties – and who must therewith face the nationalist charges of disloyalty to nation and tribe. No less is the note heard in *Discipleship* which, far from focusing simply on 'the individual Christian', is all about *participation* in the life of the Christ who calls, and about obedient sharing in his ministry of solidarity with the needy and the forgiveness of sins. 'Discipleship is being bound to the suffering Christ' (*D* 89), the Christ who suffers as vicarious representative for the world, and the world's suffering must fall upon the church community as well. 'The community of Jesus Christ vicariously represents the world before God by following Christ under the cross' (*D* 90). God is a God who *bears* and so *bearing* constitutes being a Christian too. This is even more intensively stated in the internal context of the community of faith in *Life Together*, which in many ways is an exposition in very concrete and practical terms of 'Christ existing as community'. While written out of the Finkenwalde experience it has a much wider kind of readership in mind, since its principles can apply to many types of community, whether seminary, congregation, parish or family.

At its core is the argument that Christian community is very different from all idealistic, romantic notions of community that in fact are products of self-centred wishes and impulses. It is a 'spiritual' (*geistliche*) as distinct from a 'physical-emotional' (*psychische*) community, one that involves seeing and accepting others in all their awkward, sinful humanity, in the mutual ministry of bearing, forbearing and forgiving:

> ... Christians must bear the burden of one another. They must suffer and endure one another. Only as a burden is the other really a brother or sister and not just an object to be controlled. The burden of human beings was even for God so heavy that God had to go to the cross suffering under it ... In suffering and enduring human beings, God maintained community with them. It is the law of Christ that was fulfilled in the cross. Christians share in this law.
>
> (*LT* 100)

The test of whether we are ready to hear God's word is whether we hear our all-too-real brother or sister.

On the one hand, Bonhoeffer's understanding of the person and work of Jesus Christ is very traditional. He uses the classic Lutheran language of Christ *extra nos* and *pro nobis*, Christ distinct from us yet for us. This is the biblical Christ, the Christ of Paul, the one who dies 'for' the ungodly, taking their place, standing in for them before God with all their sins so that they might stand with his righteousness. He is unreservedly free for humankind in his costly grace. We can imagine Bonhoeffer singing with gusto Charles Wesley's Ascensiontide hymn:

> See! The heaven its Lord receives,
> yet he loves the earth he leaves:
> though returning to his throne,
> still he calls mankind his own.

What is distinctive, though, is Bonhoeffer's version of Christ in *wholly* relational terms, and of the work of Christ as the creation of a new human community, without reference to inner 'spiritual experiences' or 'religious states of mind' or even 'being born again' as a new kind of individual. It is all about a God who in Christ takes our place, we in turn taking the places of others in a new kind of humanity. But having recast theology within the framework of human sociality, where does this process end? Can the question of Christ be confined to the community of the Church, or even to the Church's relation to society, or does it also run into the widest reaches of social life, Church or no Church?

This-worldliness

In 1928, while still an assistant pastor in Barcelona, Dietrich Bonhoeffer gave an address on 'Basic Questions of a Christian Ethic' in which he declared: 'The earth remains our mother, just as God remains our father, and only those who remain true to the mother are placed by her into the father's arms. Earth and its distress – that is the Christian's Song of Songs' (*BBNY* 378). From this youthful statement right to his prison writings, remaining 'true to the earth',[2] or what he later called 'this-worldliness', is the third of Bonhoeffer's most persistent themes.

In part this was an expression of his personality. Bonhoeffer enjoyed life and all that this world has to offer to body, mind and spirit: nature, sports, books and culture, above all music (even his Bechstein piano had to accompany him from Berlin to his London manse in 1933), good food and wine (not to mention tobacco – he would have found today's anti-smoking regimes a sore trial). The love and support of family, friends and fiancée were everything to him, so much so as to make him a very demanding person at times, and moreover a puzzle to himself. And it is to his fiancée Maria von Wedemeyer that he writes, after a recent visit from her in prison, 'What does belonging together mean, if not sharing everything with each other?', wondering at her implicit sadness that he cannot quite fathom (*LL* 188). Gratitude and longing, hope and anxiety pour out in the verses he wrote in prison, especially the moving poem 'Who am I?' Bonhoeffer is never more than very human, but lived human life to the full.

Bonhoeffer's 'this-worldliness', however, is not only a personal predilection for 'making the most of life'. It is a specific theological perspective in which the created world, including the human, is a world that God loves in all its creatureliness, and *to which* God *comes*. In a sermon preached in Berlin in 1932, Bonhoeffer spoke strikingly on the verse in the Lord's Prayer, 'thy kingdom come on earth'. The Church's ancient prayer, he says, tends to be prayed either in other-worldly fashion (seeking God by leaving the world behind) or in secularist fashion (despising God to find the world). Neither way is successful:

> The man who loves God, loves him as the lord of the earth, as it is; the man who loves the earth, loves her as God's earth. The man who loves the kingdom of God, loves it precisely because it is *God's* kingdom, and he loves it as God's kingdom *on earth*. The reason is simple – the king of that kingdom is the creator and sustainer of the earth.[3]

The sinful earth now bears the curse, but Christ has come in human flesh and borne that curse on the cross. This has a stark bearing on our attitude to our contemporary world:

> When we pray for the coming of the kingdom, we can only pray for it coming on earth, this earth, not some earth that we have transfigured. We cannot pray for the coming of the kingdom on earth if we try to flee from the cares and responsibilities of earth, this earth. Our prayer forces us into the company of the children of this world, it commits us to accept the facts of this earth, its care, its hunger, its death. It places us in complete solidarity with our fellow-men in their evil and their guilt. When we pray for the coming

of the kingdom of God we stand together with the world. We grind our teeth with them and with them clench our fists. This is no time for lonely piety.[4]

In the same period, Bonhoeffer's lectures on creation were stressing how the Genesis accounts depict humankind being created in the image of God yet 'formed out of earth'. Humanity's origin 'is in a piece of earth'. Our bond with the earth belongs to our essential being. The earth is our mother, it is God's earth out of which man is taken. Bonhoeffer then disputes the dichotomy between 'body' and 'soul' that denigrates the former:

> It is God's earth out of which humankind is taken ... The body is not the prison, the shell, the exterior of a human being; instead a human being is a human body. A human being does not 'have' a body or 'have' a soul; instead a human being 'is' body and soul. The human being in the beginning really is the body, is one – just as Christ is wholly his body and the church is the body of Christ. People who reject their bodies reject their existence before God the creator.
>
> (*CF* 76)

Bonhoeffer at this time is thus protesting against both a falsely 'spiritual' flight from this world into some future kingdom, and a false 'spiritualizing' of human existence itself. We discover our essential humanity not by disembodying ourselves, rather by accepting our bodies as the Creator's intention and gift. To meet God in the world we do not have to make it something other than it is in its earthiness, its materiality, still less turn aside from its need and suffering. For God comes to this very world that is in the first place God's creation. Bonhoeffer is above all a theologian of Advent, of hopeful and expectant waiting for God's *coming into* instead of our *getting out of* our world, as seen in his sermons and meditations for that season in the Church's year.[5]

From 1933, during the intensity of the Church Struggle and the fraught years at Finkenwalde, 'this-worldliness' may seem to have retreated in Bonhoeffer's mind as the issue of the integrity of the Church came to the fore. To an extent it did. *Discipleship* stresses single-minded obedience to Jesus Christ, the 'extraordinary' nature of the Christian life, the sharp separation between the Church and the world. But the very fact that it was the *visible* nature of the Church that was at issue – the way it was led as well as what it preached, and above all who could belong to it (a racial Church or an inclusive one?) – meant that what was taking place was a very public struggle for a place on this earth, not a flight into a spiritual 'beyond'. For Bonhoeffer, 'this-worldliness' returned more explicitly to the fore as the possibilities for church activity diminished in the face of even more repressive state action, and with the coming of war and his entry into the resistance. Here the dominant questions become those of Christian ethics in a world that seems bent on self-destruction, and what constitutes responsible action for a citizen faced with politicized evil on such a demonic scale.

It is in this context that Bonhoeffer sets about his *Ethics*, a crucial section of which is titled 'Ultimate and Penultimate Things'. Here he is trying to correct a certain tendency in Protestant preaching. For the Reformation tradition, salvation – justification – is by God's grace alone, received by faith alone. This is the ultimate truth, the 'last word' of the gospel. Bonhoeffer fully affirms this – he is a good Lutheran! But the temptation of Protestant piety has been to make this 'last word' the *only* word people need to hear: the world is going to rack and ruin so hear the message while there is time! Forget about trying to make the world a better place! At best it can only be held together for a time by brute force and the sword – let it go! On this showing, the Church has nothing to say about life in the world as it is. But, Bonhoeffer argues: Is there not a 'penultimate' word as well as an ultimate one? Does the command of God not give direction for worldly life? Does not the gospel need some preparatory word? Jesus himself needed John the Baptist as a 'forerunner'. At the very least, conditions of human life that prevent or make difficult the reception of the message of grace, such as slavery, hunger, disease and oppression, must be combated. The hungry need bread, the homeless roofs over their heads, the dispossessed justice, the lonely fellowship and slaves freedom. 'To bring bread to the hungry is preparing the way for the coming of grace' (*E* 163). The penultimate, or 'thing before the last', is therefore important, and so Bonhoeffer proceeds to consider such areas as 'the natural', the right to bodily life and its freedom, reproduction and nascent life, suicide, and the natural rights of the life of the mind. This represents a proper theological safeguarding of 'this-worldliness'.

Thinking in one realm

A very significant section in Bonhoeffer's *Ethics* is a critique of what he calls 'thinking in terms of two realms'. More positively, perhaps, we can describe so much of Bonhoeffer's thought as attempting to engage with life as one inclusive sphere of thought and responsibility. When in Tegel prison, he was reputedly once asked by a fellow inmate how it was that he, a pastor, had evidently become entangled in political matters to the displeasure of the state. Bonhoeffer replied that if one day he saw a car careering down the street obviously driven by a madman, he would not just stand watching to see how many victims would require his good offices to conduct their funerals, but would feel bound to jump onto the running board of the car and try to wrench the steering wheel out of the madman's grasp. In other words, he felt that being a pastor in no way excused him from what, as a human being and a German citizen, he owed in responsibility to other human beings as citizens. In Nazi Germany there were many Germans, including devout Christians and pastors, who were not Nazis and who even strongly disapproved of Hitler. But few of them would have considered it their Christian responsibility to try and wrest the wheel of state from the dictator. That was the job of politicians, not religious people, least of all pastors. The old Lutheran dichotomy between the spiritual realm and the political, the Church and the state, the gospel and the law, still ran very deep.

As we have seen in Chapter 1, in April 1933, very soon after the Nazi revolution, Bonhoeffer presented to his church authorities in Berlin a paper on 'The Church and the Jewish Question' that even at that early stage raised novel questions for traditional Lutheranism: the need to care for victims of injustice regardless of whether or not they belonged to the Church since 'the church has an unconditional obligation to the victims of any ordering of society, even if they do not belong to the Christian community'; the possibility of questioning the state's actions as to their compatibility with its mandate to safeguard justice; and, most provocatively of all, whether the time might come when a council of the Church might have to consider putting 'a spoke in the wheel' of the state in view of the state's failing in its duty to protect the rights of all in society. Clearly, here Bonhoeffer was instinctively rejecting a 'two-realms' notion of responsibility that would set religious duty over against political responsibility, or confine church concern only to the suffering of Christians, or indeed limit the Church's responsibility to remedial 'ambulance' work as distinct from prevention of oppression and injustice. That is why he felt ashamed of the failure of even the Confessing Church leadership to speak out after the atrocities of *Kristallnacht* in 1938 (see p. 18).

But while Bonhoeffer's rejection of a two-realms mentality may have been instinctive, it was also seeking definite theological formulation. We find that having in *Discipleship* set out uncompromisingly the 'narrow way' of following Jesus, of obeying his concrete commands, of bearing the cross and dying with him, Bonhoeffer brings us at the end of that same book to the discovery that this way is but the *beginning* of a new kind of life. The Jesus whom we follow is the incarnate Son of

God in whom the divine image is restored in humankind, and in fellowship with whom the divine image is restored also in us who follow. The Christ with whom we are in solidarity is the one who has made himself one with all humankind. Thereby we ourselves are called to a new kind of solidarity.

> In Christ's incarnation all of humanity regains the dignity of bearing the image of God. Whoever from now on attacks the least of the people attacks Christ, who took on human form and who in himself has restored the image of God for all who bear a human countenance. In community with the incarnate one, we are once again given our true humanity. With it, we are delivered from the isolation caused by sin, and at the same time restored to the whole of humanity . . . Since we know ourselves to be accepted and borne within the humanity of Jesus, our new humanity now also consists in bearing the troubles and sins of all others.
>
> (*D* 285)

So the narrow defile of discipleship leads into a new panorama, of solidarity with all humanity under the universal 'philanthropy' of God (Titus 3.4) revealed in the incarnation of Christ.

Christocentricity, sociality and this-worldliness thus fold together in the single sphere of God's love and human responsibility. This sets the framework for Bonhoeffer's *Ethics*, which he had always considered would be his major work. Here the attack on thinking in terms of two realms is explicit and sustained. His target is wider than the traditional Lutheran dichotomy, however, being any division of reality into a 'sacred' and a 'secular' sphere, each claiming autonomy over against the other:

> As long as Christ and the world are conceived as two realms bumping against and repelling each other, we are left with only the following options. Giving up on reality as a whole,

either we place ourselves in one of the two realms at the same time, wanting Christ without the world or the world without Christ – and in both cases we deceive ourselves. Or we try to stand in the two realms at the same time, thereby becoming people in eternal conflict ...

(*E* 58)

There are, he says, not two realities, but only one, 'and that is God's reality revealed in Christ in the reality of the world' (*E* 58).

In *Ethics* Bonhoeffer's framework thus remains firmly Christological, only it is less the Christ of the Gospels (as in *Discipleship*) who is now in view and more the cosmic Christ of Paul, the one in whom 'all things in heaven and on earth were created' and in whom 'all things hold together' (Colossians 1.16, 17). Or we might say that whereas in the Christology lectures of 1933 the focus is on Christ the centre of human existence, here in *Ethics* what is in view is the whole sweep of that human existence of which Christ is the centre. In each and every earthly and human reality and relationship, one has to reckon with Jesus Christ, and faith and obedience to Jesus Christ lead the believer into limitless engagement with earthly responsibilities, for Christ is the Lord of all. This means that each and every relationship is one in which Christ is to take form. Much of the *Ethics* attempts to explore what this means for the 'normal' social relationships and responsibilities such as home, work and government, and crucial here is Bonhoeffer's notion of 'deputyship' or 'vicarious representative action' as expressing the structure of responsible life.[6] For example, a parent is a 'deputy' for his or her children, acting for them and caring for them and even suffering for them. A parent is not an isolated individual but combines in him- or herself 'the selves of a number of human beings'. So too in all spheres of human life people are called to act as 'deputies', taking responsibility for others. Jesus is the deputy par excellence who took responsibility for all humankind to the point of the cross. Here is another level at which Bonhoeffer links Christocentricity and sociality, only now it extends far beyond the bounds of the Church.

It is not hard to see Bonhoeffer's tense context of involvement in the resistance just beneath the surface here. He had moved a long way out of all traditional and conventional churchly notions of responsibility. He was no longer acting in the usual role of a Lutheran pastor, or for that matter as a pacifist idealist, but as a German citizen alongside other citizens of diverse confessional beliefs or none, in a desperate bid to salvage justice in an unprecedentedly hideous situation – a venture moreover highly ambiguous according to normal ethical lights. Was he still within the realm of Christ in this twilight zone of conspiracy, camouflage, deceit and eventual violence? There is no more searchingly provocative passage in *Ethics* than where Bonhoeffer faces the fact that 'responsible action' for others may in fact incur guilt – but refusal to take such action in order to preserve one's supposed personal innocence could incur even greater guilt. Jesus entered into the solidarity of the guilt of others and bore it to the cross, and does this by his selfless love – which paradoxically shows him free of sin. 'Now in this sinless-guilty Jesus Christ all vicarious representative responsible action [deputyship] has its origin' (*E* 275). Bonhoeffer, knowing more than most other Germans of the time the extent of the evils being committed in his country's name, knew also which form of guilt he would choose, and that, 'Because of Jesus Christ, the essence of responsible action intrinsically involves the sinless, those who act out of selfless love, becoming guilty' (*E* 276). At this point, *Ethics* still incomplete and arrest drawing near, Bonhoeffer's fusion of Christocentricity, sociality and this-worldliness is evidently reaching its climax.

3

The prison theology:
'religionless Christianity'

The 'fragmentary' nature of Bonhoeffer's prison theology should not be exaggerated. We may not be presented with an overall, carefully constructed argument moving coherently from stage to stage and an eventual conclusion, and we may at times have to sort out some paradoxical or even apparently inconsistent notions. Letters penned secretly amid the hazards of prison life, the writing frequently interrupted by air raids, often dealing with personal matters and reflections on all manner of topics other than theology, may not make for the most coherent reading. But neither is it a matter of totally random, disconnected thoughts. The letters are often quite lengthy, the theological sections tightly argued and clearly the fruit of much hard thinking (and even, in prison, reading). Arguments in one letter are often rehearsed again later, sometimes developed further. Eberhard Bethge was able to respond to a number of them and put his own questions to Bonhoeffer, and so a clandestine dialogue continued between the two friends.

The critique of 'religion'

'Religion' had never featured much in Bonhoeffer's vocabulary, so that when in his prison letters, beginning with the one to Bethge on 30 April 1944, he launches into criticism of 'religion' as an outdated form of Christianity, he is not exactly retracting a previously cherished tenet. Karl Barth's early criticism of 'religion' as understood in Liberal Protestantism – a way of humankind showing off its better side so as to prove its closeness and likeness to God – had marked Bonhoeffer for life. The God of Jesus Christ is not interested in human religiosity, which gets in the way of grace, faith and the cross, but rather in the whole of our humanness and its creation anew.

In his prison letters, however, Bonhoeffer develops his own critique of 'religion'. He sees it as a way of thinking 'metaphysically' – that is, seeing what is real as primarily lying beyond this world and our experience. 'Religion' imagines God as the answer to our problems when human powers fail, as in the ancient Greek or Roman dramas when the plot was on the point of disaster and a 'god' came to the rescue, brought on stage by a mechanical contrivance, the deus ex machina. 'Religion' thinks of God as supplying an answer to whatever human knowledge cannot for the moment, at any rate, explain (what is popularly called 'the God of the gaps'). 'Religion' is a matter of the inward, private life of the individual insulated from social and public affairs. Humankind, suggests Bonhoeffer, has now reached a stage of maturity, of responsibility for itself, such that people today *cannot* be 'religious' without betraying their essential humanity. But what is more, Christianity, however much it may have worn the guise of 'religion' for two thousand years, is *not* a religion but, according to the Bible, something very different. It is not a seeking after God 'beyond' this life, but an encounter with God who is the 'Beyond in the midst of life'. For example:

> It is said to be decisive that in Christianity the hope of the resurrection is proclaimed, and that in this way a genuine religion of redemption has come into being. Now the emphasis is on that which is beyond death's boundary. And precisely here is where I see the error and the danger. Redemption now means being redeemed out of sorrows, hardships, anxieties and longings, out of sin and death, in a better life beyond. But should this really be the essence

of the proclamation of Christ in the Gospels and Paul?
I dispute this. The Christian hope of resurrection is
different from the mythological in that it refers people to
their life on earth in a wholly new way, and more sharply
than the Old Testament.

(*LPP* 27.06.44)

We can therefore be quite clear what Bonhoeffer is rejecting
in his quest for a 'religionless Christianity': religion conceived
as some special 'area' of life (the 'inward' or 'spiritual' realm in
contrast with the totality of life including the bodily); religion
as a matter of individual piety as distinct from public and social
responsibility; God as the 'extra' to human life who is called
on when people can no longer cope; God as the 'explanation'
of natural phenomena that cannot apparently be explained in
scientific terms. In short, God as 'beyond' what we know, experience and are able to do. Such a God is disappearing from the
world, although more and more 'religious' effort is expended
on trying still to find room for this God either in the innermost
recesses of the self, on the boundaries of life or even beyond
those boundaries on the far side of death. This religious effort,
Bonhoeffer is saying, is futile. We must recognize that such
a God has been almost completely edged out of the world by
humankind's coming of age. But is this only the consequence
of full-grown human autonomy, dating from the triumph of
human reason in the eighteenth-century 'Enlightenment'? In
one of his most paradoxical, haunting passages Bonhoeffer dares
to suggest that somehow God's own plan is at work in encourag-
ing human maturity:

And we cannot be honest, unless we recognize that we have
to live in the world – '*etsi deus non daretur*' ['as if God
were not given']. And this is precisely what we do recognize
– before God! God himself compels us to recognize it.
Thus our coming of age leads us to a truer recognition of
our situation before God. God would have us know that

we must live as those who manage their lives without God. The same God who is with us is the God who forsakes us (Mark 15.34!) . . . The same God who makes us live in the world without the working hypothesis of God, is the God before whom we stand continually. Before God, and with God, we live without God. God consents to be pushed out of the world and onto the cross, God is weak and powerless in the world, and in precisely this way, and only so, is at our side and helps us.

(*LPP* 16.07.44)

So Bonhoeffer sees the growth of human autonomy and maturity as neither the end of faith nor of God, rather an opportunity to rediscover the truly biblical God, the God of Jesus as pictured in the Gospels. God's 'transcendence' (that is, the way God is surpassingly different from and greater than the world and ourselves) has been wrongly taught to mean a kind of divine apartness, invisibility, inaccessibility, a sheer 'beyondness'. In contrast:

God is the beyond in the midst of our lives. The church does not stand at the point where human powers fail, at the boundaries, but in the centre of the village. That's the way it is in the Old Testament, and in this sense we don't read the New Testament nearly enough in the light of the Old.

(*LPP* 30.04.44)

God is thus a transforming presence encountered within, not sought outside, human daily experience and so-called 'secular' responsibilities; not in the retreat from science but in its reception and responsible use:

Here too, God is not a stopgap. We must recognize God not only where we reach the limits of our possibilities. God wants to be recognized in the midst of our lives, in life and not only in dying, in health and strength and not only in suffering, in action and not only in sin. The ground for this lies in the revelation of God in Jesus Christ. God is the centre of life, and doesn't just 'turn up' when we have unsolved problems to be solved. Seen from the centre of life, certain questions fall away completely and likewise the answers to such questions . . .

(*LPP* 29.05.44)

This, argues Bonhoeffer, is what is significant about Jesus. Jesus does not call a person to 'religion' but to life. He does not go out of his way to demonstrate that people 'need God' by revealing that they have hitherto unrecognized 'needs' in their souls, but he calls all people, healthy and sick, not only those on the edges (such as harlots and tax collectors) but those flourishing with power, into his messianic way. 'Jesus claims all of human life, in all its manifestations, for himself and for the kingdom of God' (*LPP* 30.06.44). In short, whereas religion depends on finding or inducing weakness in people, the God of Jesus Christ can encounter people as they are, even in their greatest strength, and invite them to *become* weak as he himself is weak in suffering love. In one of the poems he wrote in prison, 'Christians and Heathens', Bonhoeffer expresses it thus:

> People go to God when they're in need,
> plead for help, pray for blessing and bread,
> for rescue from their sickness, guilt and death.
> So do they all, all of them, Christians and heathens.
>
> People go to God when God's in need,
> find God poor, reviled, without shelter or bread,
> see God devoured by sin, weakness and death.
> Christians stand by God in God's own pain.
>
> God goes to all people in their need,
> fills body and soul with God's own bread,
> goes for Christians and heathens to Calvary's death
> and forgives them both.

(*LPP* 3/174)

There are thus important clues on the direction Bonhoeffer's thought was taking in seeking a 'religionless' or 'worldly' Christianity. Moreover, we have the nearest thing to a distillate of what he wanted to write at greater length, in the form of his 'Outline for a Book'. This book would have been a comparatively short work of three chapters, the first of which, 'A Stocktaking of Christianity', was to rehearse the theme of 'the coming of age' of humankind and the futile attempt to maintain Protestant Christianity 'as a religion'. The notes on the second chapter include these highly condensed but revealing indications of what the theological heart of a 'religionless Christianity' would comprise:

> Who is God? Not primarily a general belief in God's omnipotence, etc. That is not a genuine experience of God but just a prolongation of a piece of the world. Encounter with Jesus Christ. Experience that here there is a reversal of all human existence, in the very fact that Jesus only 'is there for others'. Jesus' 'being-for-others' is the experience of transcendence! Only through this liberation from self, through this 'being-for-others' unto death, do omnipotence, omniscience, and omnipresence come into being. Faith is participating in this being of Jesus (becoming human, cross, resurrection). Our relationship to God is no 'religious' relationship to some highest, most powerful and best being imaginable – that is no genuine transcendence. Instead, our relationship to God is a new life in 'being there-for-others', through participation in the being of Jesus. The transcendent is not the infinite, unattainable tasks, but the neighbour within reach in any given situation.
>
> (*LPP* 4/187)

This is the basis on which Bonhoeffer envisages a new interpretation of the traditional Christian doctrines, all the way from creation to the last things, to be attempted, together with a possible revision of, for example, the Apostles' Creed. But it is not only theology and doctrine that Bonhoeffer calls to be revised. The third chapter would look at the life of the Church in quite concrete terms:

> The church is church only when it is there for others. As a first step it must give away all its property to those in need. The clergy must live solely on the free-will offerings of the congregations, and perhaps be engaged in some secular vocation. The church must participate in the worldly tasks of life in the community – not dominating, but helping and serving. It must tell people in every calling what a life with Christ is, what it means 'to be there for others'.
>
> (*LPP* 4/187)

Such proposals alone would indeed mean a radical departure for a body like the German Protestant Church, traditionally supported by the state-administered 'church tax' and with its clergy (whose training Bonhoeffer wishes to reform) still a privileged class in society. But the fact that Bonhoeffer heads this third chapter 'Conclusion' indicates that such practical matters of church life are not for him a mere postscript to the 'real' issues of a 'religionless Christianity', but form its essential expression. Such was Bonhoeffer the radical, as regards both the thought and life of the Christian Church in the future.

Present-day readers will want to join in the dialogue with Bonhoeffer with their own questions, and what follows in the rest of this chapter are simply my own suggestions for developing an understanding of what Bonhoeffer was aiming at. This perspective comes from, first, identifying the continuities with the elements of Bonhoeffer's earlier theology; second, discerning the new configurations of these elements; and, third, noting the new (or nearly new) elements that have entered into the prison thought and how these shape the emerging new pattern of his theology.

Continuities with the elements of Bonhoeffer's earlier theology

Christocentricity

In Bonhoeffer's prison letters Jesus Christ remains the definitive revelation of who God is, as much as in his earliest Barthian phase and the writing of *Discipleship*.

> All that we may rightly expect from God, and ask him for, is to be found in Jesus Christ. The God of Jesus Christ has nothing to do with what God, as we imagine him, could do and ought to do. If we are to learn what God promises, and what he fulfils, we must persevere in quiet meditation on the life, sayings, deeds, sufferings and death of Jesus. In Jesus God has said Yes and Amen to it all, and that Yes and Amen is the firm ground on which we stand.
>
> (*LPP* 21.08.44)

As stated in the 'Outline for a Book', it is encounter with Jesus and participation in his 'existence for others' that constitutes encounter with the transcendent God. Jesus Christ remains the 'centre' of human existence – and is the central question, 'Who . . . ?'

Sociality

Bonhoeffer's understanding of authentic human existence as social, not individualistic, remains fundamental. A negative feature of interpreting 'in a religious sense' is, he states, to speak individualistically. The focus of the gospel of justification by grace through faith as expounded by Paul is not about an individualistic salvation but about the establishment of the sole righteousness of *God*, which means God's new community of righteousness on earth, 'that God makes peace with humankind and that God's kingdom is drawing near' (*LPP* 3/145). It is the welfare of the wider community – 'the city where I have sent you into exile' (Jeremiah 29.7) – that is to be sought, not one's private satisfaction:

Events and circumstances may arise that take precedence over our wishes and our rights. Then, not in embittered and barren pride, but consciously yielding to divine judgement, we shall prove ourselves worthy to survive by identifying ourselves generously and selflessly with the whole community and the suffering of our fellow human beings.

(LPP 3/145)

This-worldliness

'What matters is not the beyond, but this world, how it is created and preserved, is given laws, reconciled and renewed. What is beyond this world is meant, in the gospel, to be there *for* this world . . .' (*LPP* 05.05.44). There is deep continuity here with Bonhoeffer's youthful emphasis on cherishing the earth as 'mother' along with God as 'father' (see p. 35), with the literally down-to-earth exposition of creation in his Berlin lectures of 1932–3 (see p. 37) and above all his 1932 sermon, 'Thy Kingdom Come on Earth' (see pp. 36–7); while the more recent explorations in *Ethics* of the significance of 'natural life' and the 'penultimate' carry a strong critique of Protestantism's tendency to neglect or dismiss the significance of worldly life on account of its fallen nature – which for all its fallenness is still under God's care and is the sphere of human responsibility. In short, Bonhoeffer had long lived with a 'worldly' faith.

Thinking in one realm

The criticism Bonhoeffer makes in his prison writings of 'metaphysical thinking', that is, the intellectual division of reality into what is immediate, tangible and knowable on the one hand and what is 'beyond' our senses, knowledge and real understanding on the other (with God located in that 'beyond'), is a determined extension of the critique he makes in *Ethics* of 'thinking in two realms'. There, he dismissed traditional dichotomies between sacred and secular, supernatural and natural, in favour of 'the indivisible whole of the divine reality' that is encountered in Christ as reconciler of the world to God, and in the world as reconciled to God in Christ. The critique of 'thinking in two realms' is now employed in several directions: as well as the upward critique of metaphysical thinking, there is in the prison writings a downward critique, a rehearsing of his earlier rejection (in the 1931–3 creation lectures, for example) of sundering human nature into 'body' and 'spirit'. Now in the prison writings, Bonhoeffer rejects the attempts of both pietistic spirituality and depth psychology to locate the 'real' person in some hidden, purely inward sphere of consciousness and conscience apart from public, bodily life, in which 'God' (or at least a person's supposed need of God) can be detected.

New configurations of the earlier elements

As well as continuing to work with these habitual themes, however, it is evident that Bonhoeffer is working out a new configuration of them. For example, his long-running Christocentricity had always carried with it the note of the suffering God, in line with Luther's 'theology of the cross' (*theologia crucis*).[1] Now it becomes even more central, with the definition of faith itself as 'sharing in the sufferings of God in the world'. It is possible to argue that Bonhoeffer here was simply projecting his own suffering onto his theology, but this is too simple an explanation, and if true would mean that we should expect a theology of despair to result. But it is a theology of hope that emerges in the prison letters. 'Only the suffering God can *help*' (my emphasis), he writes on 16 July 1944. If we are prompted to ask, 'Help to do what?' the answer will be along the lines of the creation of a new human community of righteousness, of mature and free responsibility – 'deputyship' – that cannot be imposed by sheer fiat but only inspired by Christ's example and sustained by his forgiveness.[2]

Overall, there is a remarkable concentration and dovetailing together of the previous main themes. In the 'Outline for a Book', this-worldliness ('God and the secular'), Christocentricity and sociality blend together in the passage cited earlier (see p. 49) on the encounter with God being the experienced trans-formation of all (!) human life in the fact that 'Jesus is there only for others'. The authentic relationship to the transcendent God is not 'religious' but participation in this 'existence for others' with Jesus. Years earlier, in *Sanctorum Communio* and *Act and Being*, we had 'Christ existing as community' as the theological definition of the Church. In the Christology lectures of 1933 we had Jesus as both boundary and centre of human existence. In *Discipleship* it is the Jesus who calls decisively to his way of the cross, and thence to a solidarity with all humankind in its suffering, whom faith trusts and obeys. Now, we hear Bonhoeffer proclaiming a Christ *forming* community irrespective of 'sacred' or 'secular' context, inside or outside the Church, and stating that being caught up into Christ's community-creating work ('existence for others') is our authentic relation to God, how God is to be met. It is above all in his understanding of God's 'transcendence' that this new, concentrated configuration is seen. The notion of transcendence that he rejects is the metaphysical one that posits 'God' in a realm of mystery beyond our knowing, comprehension and experience. In contrast, God is the 'Beyond in the midst' and, 'The transcendental is not infinite and unat-tainable tasks, but the neighbour who is within reach in any given situation.' But even here there is a retrieval of earlier thought. For example, in a sermon preached ten years earlier in London on Trinity Sunday 1934 Bonhoeffer had spoken of 'mystery':

> *[M]ystery does not mean simply not knowing something.* The greatest mystery is not the most distant star; to the contrary, the closer something is to us, the better we know it, the more mysterious it becomes to us. The person furthest away from us is not the most mysterious to us, but rather the neigh-bour ... The very deepest mystery is when two persons grow so close to each other that they *love* each other.
>
> (*L* 361)

We must find God in what we know, not what we do not know, says Bonhoeffer in prison. This relocating of transcendence from the boundary to the centre of human life, from what is unknowable to the life of relationships, can be seen as the furthest Bonhoeffer was able to reach in attempting to overcome 'thinking in two realms'.

New elements in the prison thought

It is equally evident that as well as replaying his long-running themes, and as well as revising their harmonic relationships, Bonhoeffer was bringing what were (for him) quite new elements into his prison thought.

Coming of age

First and foremost is that of the 'coming of age' of humankind, a process he identified as having begun in the later Middle Ages and of which the European Enlightenment was the greatest landmark, and that is now nearing completion. '"God" as working hypothesis, as stop-gap for our embarrassments, has become superfluous (as indicated previously)' (*LPP* 4/187). It is often asked how someone who was enduring, of all things, Nazi imprisonment could possibly talk of humankind's 'coming of age' and of being able to 'manage without God'. But by the world's coming of age or maturity Bonhoeffer was not meaning growth in moral stature, any more than a person who reaches the age of majority at 18 automatically becomes a more moral person. Maturity, or autonomy, means being fully accountable for one's own actions, taking responsibility for oneself, and not always looking for someone else to give advice or solve one's daily problems (or to blame for one's troubles). It does seem that previously Bonhoeffer had not really taken this concept of humanity's coming of age seriously, nor the major theological challenge it presented to Western Christianity. Hitherto he had launched his theological enterprises from within the sphere of the recognized disciplines of biblical, philosophical and systematic theology. From that vantage point he was deeply conscious of how theology needed to challenge the neo-pagan horrors of Nazism. Now, he is to work not from within a church seminary, a manse study or a Benedictine monastery, but from within a prison cell. In fact the secularity of his context had already been growing through involvement in the resistance and new-found levels of collaboration with the 'unchurched' members of his family circle. He was becoming more aware that the world was not simply to be divided between Christians and Nazis, and that the post-Nazi world would pose quite new challenges for a Church that was neither being persecuted nor assured of a privileged place in society. Already in *Ethics* he had written on 'Christ and good people', that is, people with a strong commitment to social responsibility but not necessarily identifying themselves as 'Christians', and in the political resistance (not least within his own family circle) he well knew of such 'good people'. The 'world come of age' is challenging him with a quite new contextual starting point for his theology, a context in which people manage without 'God'. He is starting not from the accepted teaching of the Church or from the Bible but from the other end of human understanding, the contemporary world in which responsible people find themselves and decide how to face their challenges.[3]

Two new intellectual sources were important stimuli for Bonhoeffer at this point. First, a fresh appreciation of the natural sciences was provided by his reading *Zum Weltbild der Physik* by Carl von Weizsäcker, which had only just appeared.[4] Previously the world of the sciences was not totally unknown to Bonhoeffer: his brother Karl-Friedrich was a distinguished physicist, his father took a scientific approach to psychiatry, both were agnostic towards religion. Nor, previously, had Bonhoeffer had any difficulty acknowledging that a scientific ('Darwinian') view of the origin and development of life on the one hand, and a theological understanding of creation on the other, were quite different exercises and not in competition with one another. This comes across clearly in his expositions of Genesis in *Creation and Fall*. Nevertheless, Bonhoeffer confesses that only now does it really come home to him how as a feature of the Western cultural landscape, 'God' has progressively become redundant, thanks in large measure to the growth of the scientific world-view. There are now only a few, fast-diminishing gaps not covered by science – unsolved mysteries – for the traditional God to hide in.

The second new stimulus was the philosopher Wilhelm Dilthey (1833–1911), who constitutes an interesting foil to Weizsäcker the physical scientist. Dilthey was a highly original and influential philosopher of history and historical method, especially as these involved the interpretation (hermeneutics) of historical texts and other artefacts. He stressed the profound difference between the 'human' sciences (of culture, art, religion, etc.) and the 'natural' sciences, and advocated an *integration* of the different kinds and levels of knowledge and discourse into a unifying 'philosophy of life' for truly *autonomous* living. Bonhoeffer several times mentions Dilthey and his eagerness to obtain more of his works. This was all of a piece with his new interest in and appreciation of nineteenth-century German intellectual achievement that he felt had been lost sight of in the social upheavals, cultural fragmentation and radical changes in thought since 1918. It was evidently the sense of *wholeness* in that tradition, represented at its clearest in Dilthey, that made such an appeal to Bonhoeffer. Dilthey's was the vision of a life that could embrace all forms of knowledge, in which all truly human values would find their place, and in which the human being would be thus fully equipped to live 'autonomously' – that is, in free responsibility for the welfare of the community and its future. This was how Bonhoeffer envisaged 'coming of age' and human 'autonomy', in the development of a 'philosophy of life'.[5]

A new kind of Church: prayer and doing justice

Faced with such an integrated and autonomous 'philosophy of life', what should be the Church's response? How does the gospel engage with such human maturity? Bonhoeffer regards with utter distaste all attempts to prove to happy, secure, contented people that they are *not* really as well as they think they are (he calls this approach 'methodism', by which he is not denigrating the followers of John Wesley but rather those forms of counselling and psychotherapy that seek to 'uncover' what is 'really' going on 'beneath' a person's conscious and outward life). Nor does he look for this integrated, autonomous life to have within it some space marked off for 'religion'. Rather, the gospel must be addressed to life *as a whole and in its wholeness*. 'Jesus claims all of human life, in all its manifestations, for himself and for the kingdom of God' (*LPP* 30.06.44); 'Jesus does not call to a new religion, but to life' (*LPP* 18.07.44). Bonhoeffer (as in *Discipleship*) refers to the Gospel story of Jesus and the rich young ruler. Jesus finds nothing wrong with the rich young ruler in his exemplary keeping of the ten commandments, and loves him for it. He simply makes a claim on him and calls him to follow him, to share with him his messianic way and his suffering. This is what Bonhoeffer means by wishing to confront mature humankind at its *strongest* point, manifesting the 'aristocracy' of the word of God in contrast to the inferiority complex of an evangelism that grubs around hoping only to find where people are weak. The Church's task is 'to tell people in every calling what a life with Christ is, what it means "to be there for others"' (*LPP* 4/187).

It is just here, however, that Bonhoeffer knows he faces a major question, namely the adequacy of the contemporary Church to meet the situation he is describing. Much of the German Church lay organizationally wrecked and morally discredited in the Third Reich years. Bonhoeffer laments that even the Confessing Church, which he himself had served so gallantly and at such cost, had in the end got no further than preserving itself against the Nazi onslaught instead of saving *the nation* from Nazism, let alone protecting the Jews and other victims from genocide. It had not really existed 'for others'. He also complains with some poignancy that Karl Barth too, after his early attack on 'religion' (for which Bonhoeffer is eternally grateful), had replaced 'religion' not so much with a living personal faith in Christ but rather with a reconstructed system of doctrine – a 'positivism of revelation' (a charge by which Barth was somewhat upset when eventually he read the published prison letters). Bonhoeffer's pointing to the familiar sight of the Church standing in the centre of the village is in ironic contrast to how religion has actually been marginalized. But how can the Church be other than an embarrassment in a world come of age, if what it has to say is meaningless, irrelevant or downright hypocritical?

As a means of conceiving a Church that is both true to the tradition of faith yet having to relearn what it means to be 'at the centre' and 'for others', Bonhoeffer several times in the prison writings turns to the ancient practice of the *disciplina arcani*: literally, 'the discipline of the secret', sometimes less accurately rendered 'the secret discipline'. In the early Church, pagans and catechumens were excluded from the central and most sacred part of the eucharistic liturgy in order, evidently, that these might be safeguarded against profane misunderstanding or abuse. Today, however, Bonhoeffer suggests that the danger of 'profanation' lies in the contemporary Church publicizing its doctrines wholesale at a time *when the Church itself hardly comprehends their meaning.* This comes out strikingly in the sermon Bonhoeffer wrote for the baptism of the son of Eberhard and Renate Bethge in May 1944. The great ancient words of Christian faith, he writes, will be pronounced over the infant, who will not know anything about it – which is in fact the situation of the Church as a whole. The great Christian themes of reconciliation, life in Christ and so forth, have become strange to Christians themselves. 'In these words and actions handed down to us we sense something totally new and revolutionary, but we cannot yet grasp it and express it. This is our own fault' (*LPP* 3/145). The Church has fought for its own self-preservation and is now incapable of taking the word of reconciliation to the world. So:

> ... the words we used before must lose their power, be silenced, and we can be Christians today in only two ways, through prayer and in doing justice among human beings. All Christian thinking, talking and organizing must be born anew, out of that prayer and action. By the time you grow up, the form of the Church will have changed considerably.
>
> (*LPP* 3/145)

'Prayer and doing justice' is how Bonhoeffer sees the way for the Church in the coming years until it discovers 'a new language, perhaps quite non-religious, but liberating and redeeming' (*LPP* 3/145), for proclaiming the word of God. But for the present it is not the verbal but rather the disciplined contemplative-and-active way that must be followed. As he puts it in the outline for his projected book, the Church in its existence for others must 'share in the secular problems of ordinary human life, not dominating, but helping and serving', and above all must follow the way of *human example* that, in contrast to abstract argument, 'gives its word emphasis and power' (*LPP* 4/187). Here, according to Bonhoeffer, in integrity and modesty the Church can once again be 'at the centre' in a world come of age. That world may no longer have need of a God in the old way, relegated to the margins or invoked to come in from 'beyond' as a last resort. It can manage its affairs without recourse to 'God'. But humankind charged with managing itself has to ask what it means to be human. 'Humankind has managed to deal with everything, only not with itself' (*LPP* 4/187). It is with that really central question for human existence, not with the remaining and diminishing 'religious' ones, that Christian faith has to engage.

The emerging new pattern of his theology – 'this is faith'

Clearly for Bonhoeffer, his prison theology was a deeply personal and existential matter. It was his own autonomy, not just that of humankind in general, that exercised him, and his own faith in God that he was struggling to understand anew. This fusion of the universally human and the personal, and of theology and personal faith, above all becomes clear in his letter to Eberhard Bethge of 21 July 1944, the day after the conspiracy came to its fateful climax in the failed assassination attempt on Hitler led by Claus von Stauffenberg. Bonhoeffer knew what his own fate was now likely to be. He reviews the course his life has led, and the decisions he has taken, and accepts their consequences without flinching. He admits that in earlier days he was impressed by the idea of 'sainthood' and thought he could acquire faith 'by trying to live a holy life', but continues:

Later on I discovered, and am still discovering to this day, that one only learns to have faith by living in the full this-worldliness of life. If one has completely renounced making something of oneself – whether it be a saint or a converted sinner or a church leader (a so-called priestly figure!), a just or unjust person, a sick or healthy person – then one throws oneself completely into the arms of God, and this is what I call this-worldliness: living fully in the midst of life's tasks, questions, successes and failures, experiences and perplexities – then one no longer takes one's own sufferings seriously, but rather the suffering of God in the world. Then one stays awake with Christ in Gethsemane. And I think this is faith, this is metanoia [repentance]. And this is how one becomes a human being, a Christian. (Cf. Jer. 45!) How should one become arrogant over successes or shaken by one's failures

when one shares in God's suffering in the life of this
world?

(LPP 20.07.44)

By 'living completely in this world' Bonhoeffer means venturing
totally in responsibility for others and answerability for one's
actions. It is at that point of abandonment, not at the place of
seeking security, that faith discovers it is held by grace. Hence
the seeming paradox of Bonhoeffer working out a 'religionless'
Christianity while continuing to pray, meditate and radiate to
those around him extraordinary joy and serenity that seems to
grow as his fate draws near. It is from the Gestapo cellars, no less,
that he writes to Maria his fiancée on 19 December 1944:

> Your prayers and kind thoughts, passages from the Bible,
> long-forgotten conversations, pieces of music, books – all
> are invested with life and reality as never before. I live in
> a great, unseen realm of whose existence I'm in no doubt.
> The old children's song about the angels says 'two to cover
> me, two to wake me', and today we grown-ups are no less
> in need of preservation, night and morning, by kindly,
> unseen powers.
>
> *(LL* 227)

These were the thoughts that he then put into verse as his
famous New Year poem, 'By gracious powers, so wonderfully
sheltered'. In line with his earlier comments about finding
God 'in what we know', these 'gracious powers', while unseen,
are signalled in very concrete experiences; and far from being
anodynes to ease the way of suffering they are assurances that
it is the way of the cross that, if trodden to the end, is the
way to life. Bonhoeffer shows no sign of doubting that the
ultimate – eternal life – is real. Death, as he puts it in his poem
'Stations on the Way to Freedom', is the final step to that freedom.
But the end is not to be anticipated within the penultimate,
not before the cup of earthly suffering (or earthly joy for that
matter) has been drunk to the very bottom.

There is an obvious temptation to conjecture what Bonhoeffer's finished book would have contained or how, if he had survived, he would have clarified and developed his thinking further in the post-war world. What is reasonably clear is that if the direction of his prison writings were maintained, he would call for a new emphasis on communities of discipleship that would concentrate on prayer and just works (the 'discipline of the secrets'), meditation and *learning anew* what faith and responsible action in society mean today. There would be a moratorium on much of the Church's public speech, especially about 'God', and a new attention to 'mystery' at the heart of life even in the most 'mundane' everyday affairs and relationships. There would be a new reverence too for the 'mysteries' of the tradition of faith. It would be a Church neither driftingly liberal, forgetting the tradition, nor fundamentalist, claiming to own the tradition with the right to impose its version on everyone. It would be a Church that included people still *hoping* to find meaning in the tradition of faith rather than brazenly declaring their confidence in the truth, yet at the same time a Church that willingly took risks for justice and peace. There would be emphasis on the power of example, on living out rather than speaking out, except where a voice was required on behalf of the voiceless in society. It would indeed be a Church 'for others' – and for the hidden God in the midst of life.

4

Bonhoeffer, the Jews and the Holocaust

The Jewish Holocaust, or *Shoah*, presents an inescapable theme for Western theology today. It is not only that the scale of the Nazis' 'final solution' – some six million Jews murdered – raises huge questions for any belief in 'theodicy' (God's justice in history). It is also the question of Christian complicity in this genocide that has come to the fore. A recent bibliography on the religious impact of the Holocaust lists some 1,500 articles and essays by both Jewish and Christian writers.[1] 'Theology after Auschwitz', often with a question mark, has become a motif of our time.

The Holocaust happened in 'Christian' Europe, admittedly at the hands of the Nazis but at a time when the churches were still alive, relatively strong and with the possibility of a powerful voice. There were individuals and organizations who helped Jews to hide or escape, and churches in Nazi-occupied countries made some bold public protests. But over the record as a whole a dark cloud hangs, especially where church leaders are concerned. On the Roman Catholic side the record of Pope Pius XII has been under grave scrutiny: did he hold back criticism for fear of Nazi assault on the Church? In German Protestantism, anti-Semitism had long been endemic. The Confessing Church leadership – for the most part anxious to distinguish its 'theological' stance from 'political' opposition to the Nazi state – stoutly rejected the imposition of the 'Aryan paragraph' that would have barred pastors of Jewish descent from holding office, but made little overt protest about the persecution of the Jews at large. Neither the famous Barmen Declaration on which the Confessing Church was founded in 1934, nor the post-war Stuttgart Declaration by its surviving leaders in October 1945, specifically mentioned the Jews and their fate.

This is serious enough. But there is a further charge, namely that the shame of the Church in face of Hitler and the extermination of Jews was not just a modern 'lapse' but the culmination of a 20-century-long history of Christian anti-Judaism that remains endemic in modern Europe. There are on record Martin Luther's infamous inflammatory injunctions to harry and expel the Jews. There were the Spanish persecutions, the medieval pogroms and expulsions. There is the tradition, dating back to the patristic period, of seeing the Church as the successor to God's rejected child or bride Israel: rejected for the most ultimately serious crime of deicide in the crucifixion of Jesus the Son of God, and therefore irretrievably guilty. Again, it is tempting to say that this represents a lapse, if a rather long-running one, of Christians and churches failing to live up to their true precepts and ideals. But the charge is in fact graver: that Christians and churches *were* living up to their 'ideals', and it is their basic precepts and doctrines themselves that are the source of the trouble; that the virus of anti-Semitism is not an infection from outside the Christian body, but arises directly from the core doctrines of the faith. Above all, the charge runs, Christology itself is the root cause. On this view, the doctrine that Jesus is the divine Son of God, the very incarnation of God, at least implicitly carries with it the rejection of Judaism by making an exclusive claim for the status of Jesus and thus an absolute distinction between him as truth and Judaism as untruth. Anti-Semitism is therefore spoken of as the 'dark side of Christology'.[2] Not only so, it is held: anti-Semitism is deeply embedded in the New Testament itself, especially in the Fourth Gospel, where the basic paradigm is of Jesus versus 'the Jews'.

In reaction to all this some Jewish and indeed Christian minds take the view that in the light of Auschwitz and what led to it, traditional Christianity is totally discredited.

There have of course been other sorts of reactions on the Christian side, and not wholly defensive or evasive either, in an attempt to face theologically the horror of the Holocaust. Probably the most well-known is Jürgen Moltmann's *The Cruci-fied God*.[3] But he too has been under attack, being seen by some as attempting to 'colonize' Auschwitz theologically for Christian benefit. There has been a resultant danger of sheer paralysis of Christian theology under the dual threat of being condemned if it tries, and condemned if it does not try, to respond with new approaches to an understanding of God, human freedom, Christ, suffering and the Jewish people.

Bonhoeffer: hero or villain?

As a German and a Christian of his time, Dietrich Bonhoeffer must stand trial like anyone else for his record during this horrendous piece of history. This is especially important for his Christian admirers, who may assume that thanks to his uncompromising stand against Hitler to the point of death, Bonhoeffer would be hailed as a hero by Jews as well. Such, however, is not quite the case. Many Jews do indeed profess an admiration for Bonhoeffer, and his theology has been appreciated and used by scholars such as Rabbi Irving Greenberg of the USA in working out a post-Auschwitz understanding of power and powerlessness, divine and human.[4] But suspicious of Christians using him as a showpiece to divert attention from the wider picture of failure, even admiring Jews also ask pertinently, 'Why were there so *few* Bonhoeffers in Nazi Germany?' Not only so, but Bonhoeffer himself is seen by others as an ethically ambiguous figure. The visitor to the Yad Vashem Holocaust Memorial in Jerusalem may well be surprised to find that, to date, there is no mention of Dietrich Bonhoeffer in the garden devoted to 'The Righteous

Among the Nations' – those non-Jews who took risks to save Jews from the Holocaust. In relation, therefore, to the overall accusations against Christianity, how does it stand with Bonhoeffer?

The standard pro-Bonhoeffer testimony would include the following points:

- Bonhoeffer made known from even before Hitler's rise to power his absolute opposition to the Nazi creed of blood, race and soil. This became clear in his ecumenical peace work and his trenchant theological opposition to the nationalist concept of 'orders of creation' that formed the religious basis of Nazi attempts to 'cleanse' Germany of 'non-Aryans'.

- At the time when many German theologians were attempting to play down the Jewishness of Jesus and the religious significance of the whole Hebraic tradition, Bonhoeffer in 1932 deliberately looked to the Old Testament, in his lectures on creation among other things. In fact he had a lifelong love of the Old Testament, especially the Psalter, which he described as 'The Prayer Book of the Bible'. His Christology lectures of summer 1933 – in the immediate wake of the Nazi revolution and amid the controversy about the 'Aryan clause' in the church constitution – deliberately and repeatedly spoke of the historical 'Jesus of Nazareth' and 'the Messiah', not just of 'the Christ'. In prison he avidly reread the Old Testament and confessed to thinking more on Old Testament lines with every passing day.

- Bonhoeffer was a stalwart, some even said fanatical, protagonist of the Confessing Church in its rejection of any imposition of the 'Aryan clause' on the church. A church that excluded people from its membership or ministry on account of their racial origin could not be the church of Jesus Christ.

- As we have seen (p. 11), early in the Nazi period (April 1933) Bonhoeffer wrote and published his paper, 'The Church and the Jewish Question'. It was a unique statement for a German

Lutheran. He sees the situation of the Jews as an urgent issue for the Church and commends three possible positive approaches to it: first, the Church can care for the victims, binding up those caught under the wheel whether or not they belong to the Church; second, the Church can question the state on whether its actions are promoting law; and, third, the Church can put a 'spoke in the wheel' of the state itself, a clear indication of the possibility of political resistance on behalf of persecuted Jews.

- Bonhoeffer stood by 'non-Aryan pastors' in the Confessing Church and helped a number to leave Nazi Germany and find refuge in Britain and elsewhere, and while in London during 1933–5 he helped many Jewish refugees. His own twin sister was married to a 'non-Aryan' Christian, Gerhard Leibholz, and so he knew at first hand the predicament of such people.

- Immediately after *Kristallnacht* in 1938, Bonhoeffer's personal reaction was of shock and revulsion (see p. 18), and was a clear expression of solidarity with the persecuted.

- Bonhoeffer took the definite decision in late summer 1940 to enter the political conspiracy against Hitler as an active as distinct from just a knowing supporter (as he had been hitherto). The prime motivation for this step was, as well as to avoid military conscription by officially serving in the *Abwehr* (military counter-intelligence), to stop Hitler's crimes – of which the onslaught on the Jews was the worst. Bonhoeffer was informed fully on the Nazi misdeeds by his brother-in-law Hans von Dohnanyi, a senior official in the Ministry of Justice, who was also the chief liaison between the military and civilian wings of the main resistance effort and personally invited Bonhoeffer into active involvement.

- One of the specific projects to which Bonhoeffer was assigned by von Dohnanyi was 'Operation 7' (see p. 22), in the wake of the first eastward transports of Jews from Berlin in late 1941.

- In his wartime *Ethics* Bonhoeffer writes strikingly:

> The historical Jesus Christ is the continuity of our history. Because Jesus Christ was the promised Messiah of the Israelite-Jewish people, the line of our forebears reaches back before the appearance of Jesus Christ into the people of Israel. Western history is by God's will inextricably bound up with the people of Israel, not just genetically but in an honest, unceasing encounter. The Jews keep open the question of Christ; they are the sign of God's free, gracious election and of God's rejecting wrath; 'see the kindness and the severity of God' (Rom. 11.22). *Driving out the Jews from the West must result in driving out Christ with them. For Jesus Christ was a Jew.*
>
> (E 105; emphases added)

- Also in *Ethics* comes a confession of guilt that Bonhoeffer evidently intended for use by the churches in the event of an overthrow of the regime. It is based paragraph by paragraph on the commands of the Decalogue. That corresponding to 'You shall not kill' states:

> The church confesses that it has witnessed the arbitrary use of brutal force, the suffering in body and soul of countless innocent people, that it has witnessed oppression, hatred and murder without raising its voice for the victims and without finding ways of rushing to help them. It has become guilty of the lives of the weakest and most defenceless brothers and sisters of Jesus Christ.
>
> (E 139)

What clearer reference could there be to what was happening in the 'final solution'?

In view of all this, Bonhoeffer would seem guaranteed to exemplify the truly Christian stance of opposition to the Holocaust, a shining counter-sign to the otherwise dark scene of Christian failure. Once Bonhoeffer is taken out of his admiring Christian circle, however, and exposed to wider view, some critical observations and questions must be faced. It is perhaps symbolic of this ambiguity that while one of the most oft-quoted aphorisms attributed to Bonhoeffer is, 'Only those who cry out for the Jews may sing Gregorian chant!', there is no sure evidence as to when, where, or even *if* he actually said this, as even his closest friend and biographer Eberhard Bethge admits.

The case *against* Bonhoeffer would run thus:

• Whatever theological views Bonhoeffer took up against Nazism, at any rate up until the early years of the regime, he followed the typical, traditional Lutheran attitude to the Jews. That 1933 essay on 'The Church and the Jewish Question' in fact spends a lot of time cautiously explaining that the Church should not be seen as interfering with the state except as a very last resort. But far more serious are the implications when Bonhoeffer states:

> Now the measures of the state towards Judaism in addition stand in a quite specific context for the church. The church of Christ has never lost sight of the fact that the 'chosen people', who nailed the redeemer of the world to the cross, must bear the curse for its action through a long period of suffering.
>
> (*NRS* 226)

He also quotes Luther, although not his most inflammatory statements. The Church, says Bonhoeffer, looks to the Jews' final homecoming – their conversion. They are a rejected people (and the Church is itself unfaithful). This section of the paper, for all the oft-quoted remarks about the possibility of putting a 'spoke in the wheel' of the unjust state, is, to say the least, an embarrassing feature on Bonhoeffer's profile.

- At about the same time as that paper, in the spring of 1933, Bonhoeffer submitted to the advice of his church superintendent not to officiate at the funeral of the Jewish father of his brother-in-law Gerhard Leibholz. While he came to regret deeply this decision, the episode shows just how equivocal he was to Jews outside the Christian community.

- In fact Bonhoeffer's 'concern for Jews' throughout the 1930s was virtually confined to 'non-Aryan Christians' especially pastors in the Confessing Church. He seems not to have had any contact with the Jewish community at large, nor personal acquaintance with any Jewish intellectuals, nor to have sought any such contact.

- Bonhoeffer's references to Jews in his writings manifest an inability or unwillingness to see Jews and Judaism as existing in their own right. While he indeed values the Old Testament he does so only through Christian eyes, with a Christocentric reading of the Genesis creation stories, the psalms and so on. He displays an assumed Christian right to co-opt the Hebrew Scriptures for Christian purposes, and shows no interest in what the texts say for themselves or how Jews read them.

- Likewise, on the question of the Jews in Europe, his exposition in *Ethics* (see p. 69) views them only in relation to Christ. Only the Jewishness of *Jesus* is of interest to him. That the Jews 'keep open the question of Christ' in Europe means that he has no interest in Jews or their rights for their own sakes.

- The actual motives for Bonhoeffer's entry into the conspiracy and his involvement in the *Abwehr* were to say the least ambiguous – as were in any case the intentions of the conspiracy as a whole. The political conspiracy around Admiral Canaris was not primarily about stopping the Holocaust, but about removing Hitler from power and then negotiating a peace so as to save Germany from utter ruin. Operation 7 may have been genuine but it saved only a handful of Jews.

The resistance to which Bonhoeffer belonged – and in a minor way as a courier to possible allies abroad – was not about saving Jews but about saving Germany.

- In that 'confession of guilt' in *Ethics* (see p. 69), there is still no specific mention of the Jews, except indirectly as 'brothers and sisters of Jesus Christ'. In any case, the references to violence, to murder of the innocents and the silence of the Church occupy only a few lines within the confession as a whole. Far more space is taken up with matters such as loss of parental discipline and family life, breakdown in sexual relations and so on.

In summary, the charges against Bonhoeffer's actions are: that at most only very cautiously did he move out of the traditional Christian negative attitude to Jews; that he restricted his concern mostly to Christians of Jewish descent; that while he was an opponent of Hitler, both in the Confessing Church and in political conspiracy, the latter involvement was mainly to save Germany from complete destruction, not to save Jews from mass murder.

Bonhoeffer in historical close-up

In face of such charges, can Bonhoeffer's reputation be salvaged without resorting to sheer 'hagiography' (i.e. turning him into an unreal 'saint')? A closer historical examination of Bonhoeffer's case results in what may appear to be a more 'modest' Bonhoeffer than some of his admirers may wish for but, equally, more deserving of recognition than blanket condemnations of 'Christian complicity' allow. He will be a Bonhoeffer located in the actual circumstances of his situation and facing the particular options open to him there and then, rather than in the privileged position that we as moralizing spectators of history enjoy more than half a century later. The following reflections are an attempt at a realistic perspective:

- That Bonhoeffer could cite, in his 1933 paper 'The Church and the Jewish Question', the traditional Lutheran view of the Jews as 'deicides' may indeed cast him in a traditional anti-Semitic light. But even assuming that he here really was supporting the conventional view as distinct from just *acknowledging* it in a presentation to church leaders, this may indicate no more than that he at that time reflected his background and upbringing. We find no similar statement by Bonhoeffer later than this, and it must therefore be asked whether it marked a position from which he moved considerably rather than one in which he stayed.

- As regards the episode of the funeral of Gerhard Leibholz's father, Bonhoeffer soon afterwards realized he had made a mistake, felt ashamed and in a letter to Leibholz begged his forgiveness.

- Certainly no purpose is served by exaggerating Bonhoeffer's role as a resister. As we have seen, he was not even a senior figure in the Confessing Church, his actual role in the resistance as a double-agent in the *Abwehr* was relatively minor, and the charges on which he was initially arrested in 1943 were also relatively minor. Bonhoeffer's significance lies less in the scale of his activities than in the fact that, even as a minor figure, it was a major step to take sides on such a huge divide. After 20 July 1944, even just to *know* there had been a plot in the making was enough to get oneself hanged. The question was not how much one was to do but whether one was going to risk any concrete involvement at all. He acted from what and where he was, with his family connections and ecumenical contacts. Bonhoeffer and others like him did act, when the majority did nothing at all.

- The motives for Bonhoeffer's involvement in the conspiracy may have been mixed, but they were a mixture of basically *good* intentions. One major ingredient was certainly his wish to have a pretext, as an *Abwehr* agent, to avoid conscription. This, by itself, does not prove his anti-Holocaust credentials.

But does that make this wish – not to serve in Hitler's uniform – any less honourable?

- Operation 7 may have been relatively small-scale, but it was undoubtedly intended to save Jews, following the first transports of Jews from Berlin in late 1941, and did so.

- The paucity of explicit references to the suffering of Jews notwithstanding, it is inconceivable that Bonhoeffer did not react with horror to what he knew was happening to Jews at large. His biblical annotations on *Kristallnacht* (see p. 18) make that clear. He was repelled by everything Hitler was doing, and it is simply impossible to imagine him averting his gaze from any aspect of those murderous policies. So when he says in 'Night Voices in Tegel', one of his 1944 prison poems, 'We saw the lie raise its head/And we did not honour the truth./We saw brethren in direst need,/And feared only our own death', there is no reason to think he did not at least include in this the onslaught on the Jews.

- Here, however, is where we come to perhaps the most sensitive point in the whole exercise: the specificity of the fate of the Jews in the totality of the 'horrorscape' that was Nazism. Many people were to claim they did not know what was happening to the Jews. Bonhoeffer knew, and knew that horrors were also happening to others – known later not to be on the scale that the Jews suffered but horrors none the less. Gypsies and homosexuals are now commonly cited among these other groups of victims, but especially in the early stages of the war, one category of people was literally foremost in the firing line: the Poles. Poland was effectively to be wiped off the map and out of history. It was what was happening in Poland, not just to Jews but to civilians at large, that was most apparent in 1939–40, the period in which Bonhoeffer eventually decided to join in the *Abwehr*-based conspiracy. He heard about what was happening to Polish villagers from at least one of his former students serving in the army there. This is not to attempt a comparison with the enormity of the European Jewish Holocaust as a whole, but simply to identify what would have been centre-stage in the consciousness of someone like Bonhoeffer in the first 12 months of the war.

- It can therefore be said that Bonhoeffer, whether or not he saw the fate of the Jews as a *unique* evil in scale and nature, would have seen what was happening to them within a framework of overall evil being committed by the Nazi regime, and it was this total picture that morally justified his involvement in conspiracy. Does this lower his moral stature? Arguably, by no means. In fact it is the anxiously enthusiastic attempts to identify the Holocaust alone as providing his motivation that are in danger of downgrading Bonhoeffer, for they come close to saying that he was *not* moved by other or earlier known Nazi crimes against humanity, and this would hardly indicate a sensitive conscience or morally aware spirit. If it takes an actual Holocaust of six million people to stir one to resistance, that is hardly a good advertisement for one's ethics.

- In all this, it is not being definitely suggested that Bonhoeffer did *not* regard the murder of the Jews as a unique evil and the prime motivation for his acts of resistance. The sure evidence we do have is that he regarded the Nazi regime as so criminally evil in its entire works, including its elimination of the Jews, that resistance and even tyrannicide were justified, and he was prepared to 'become guilty for others'. There is then even no problem in admitting, for example, that when Bonhoeffer speaks in *Ethics* of the Church being answerable for 'the lives of the weakest and most defenceless brothers and sisters of Jesus Christ' (see p. 69), he may not even have been speaking specifically of the Jews. We may be quite sure he was *including* them in this description. The fact that in his time and place, given all else that was happening, he does not necessarily accord them unique or specific mention indicates no weakness. Hitler was doing enough to horrify anyone of the slightest moral responsibility. And in any case Bonhoeffer had already shown in the *Ethics*, in his remark on an expulsion of Jews from Europe, what was his view.

- Furthermore, on the question of whether Bonhoeffer was more concerned to save Germany than to save the Jews, both the ethics and the practicalities of the conspiracy need to be examined very closely. Yes, it was Bonhoeffer who through Bishop Bell sought mediation with the British government and the allies: would a non-Nazi German government be recognized by the allies as a negotiating partner? There were indeed some, politically very conservative and even anti-Semitic in attitude, for whom this was the paramount aim. But for others, Bonhoeffer included, this was not the *entire goal* of the attempt on Hitler. For them, the objective was the removal of the Nazi state and all its terror apparatus and evil policies, so that Germany might be morally no less than politically cleansed and a new beginning be made with the family of nations. This was so for Bonhoeffer, as he made clear in his secret meeting in Sweden at the end of May 1942 with Bishop George Bell.

A final judgement on Bonhoeffer's moral standing in relation to the fate of the Jews will depend on how far one wishes to abstract the Holocaust from the total historicity of evil under Hitler and to ignore the concrete particularities of the day-by-day engagement of Bonhoeffer in that history. If he began as a traditional Lutheran vis-à-vis the Jewish question, the issue then is the direction in which he journeyed from there – not the extent of his intellectual and cultural confinement but how, given that localization, he acted in it. We do not need to pretend that Bonhoeffer was better than he was, nor to turn him retroactively into the angel we feel that we require in order to improve the Christian record of that time. He was a person of his time and a product of his culture and history, but the claim made on his behalf is that nevertheless he was able to transcend these limitations in civic courage and responsible action.

Bonhoeffer the theologian: a Christology of solidarity

So much for the historical side, but what of the theological? Dietrich Bonhoeffer was in many respects a classically orthodox Lutheran theologian, as shown in his 1933 lectures on Christology. Was he, therefore, also guilty of promoting the 'dark side of Christology' that allegedly separates Christianity from the rest of humanity as a whole?

To recap briefly on those Christology lectures, Bonhoeffer prefers to speak not of 'incarnation' as a general term, but of 'the incarnate one': not the what, or how of incarnation, but *who is the man Jesus, the Jew* who is God incarnate, the Word made flesh, human. It is precisely in Jesus' utmost humanness that God is present, incognito. He is the humiliated one and also the exalted one, in solidarity with and glorifying the whole of humanity. Thus for Bonhoeffer the uniqueness of Jesus Christ does not make him the exclusive preserve of any one section of humanity. As we have seen (pp. 40–1), at the end of *Discipleship* Bonhoeffer presents Jesus Christ as the one who bears the image of God in human form and does this precisely in his solidarity with all humankind, calling his followers into a like solidarity. This unitary view is carried still further in the *Ethics*, where Jesus is seen as the one who does not *make* others guilty but takes their guilt upon himself, and who calls all people 'into the fellowship of guilt'. What is taking place in Bonhoeffer is a fusion of Christology and ethics. Bonhoeffer's Christ is one not of separation but of overcoming barriers. It is the condescension of God in the human Jesus, in loving solidarity with the whole human race, that is operative here, not the denigration of one section, whether Jew or Gentile in the interests of another, or even of the Christian. It is a Christology that in turn motivates solidarity with others and especially the afflicted. Christology here is thus not an abstraction from the situation, or exclusivism, nor is it paralytic of responsibility. Quite the reverse: it motivates engagement and solidarity and it nerves for action. Here Bonhoeffer can be seen as pioneering a way forward towards a Christology that liberates, that celebrates God's reconciling oneness with all humankind. It can therefore be argued that, far from merely reinforcing the 'dark' side of Christology and its destructive potential, Bonhoeffer both retrieves the classical tradition and shows how, without distortion, it can be read and used in a way very different from its allegedly exclusivist, anti-Semitic and otherwise oppressive tendencies. Bonhoeffer's theology and his detailed history illuminate each other, and there emerges an impressive correlation between the kind of actions he was undertaking and the theological understanding that integrated them with faith, placing the human subject in a proper and just perspective and unfolding the theology into new possibilities.

What we can be sure of is that Bonhoeffer would have had no objection to being put on moral trial in this respect or any other. Let the final word be his testimony to Bishop Bell at their poignant last meeting in Sweden in 1942. Bell later recalled:

> Deeply committed as he was to the plan for elimination [of Hitler], he was not altogether at ease about such a solution. 'There must be punishment by God', he said. 'We do not want to escape repentance.' The elimination itself, he urged, must be understood as an act of repentance. 'Oh, we have to be punished. Christians do not wish to escape repentance or chaos, if God wills to bring it on us. We must endure this judgement as Christians.'[5]

5

Pursuing Bonhoeffer

During the 1970s a certain German professor of theology was reputed always to begin his first seminar with new students by throwing at them the proposition: 'Theology is a purely academic discipline to be pursued for its own sake, and has no bearing on daily life.' His object of course was to get the students' minds working and to discuss the nature of what they would be studying. But he was also playing a private game, of placing a bet with himself on how long it would be (this time!) for the name of Dietrich Bonhoeffer to be thrown into the ring in contradiction of his statement. Certainly, if for nothing else, more than 60 years after his death Dietrich Bonhoeffer is generally known as 'the theologian who opposed Hitler', evidently supplying theology with a valid entry ticket into public affairs.

In fact that professor's method was very much in line with Bonhoeffer's own teaching style. Students often found his lectures gripping, but he himself much preferred the seminar method, certainly at the Finkenwalde seminary, whether in the classroom or, weather permitting, on the nearby sand dunes. A favourite trick was to propose a quite problematic or even outrageous thesis for debate, and only when the resulting discussion seemed to be getting out of hand or completely stuck, to come in with an alternative way of looking at the question. This is not to say that in his writings Bonhoeffer uses the same method and intends only to provoke, for characteristically every word put by him on paper is carefully weighed.

But if one is not made to think very hard when reading Bonhoeffer then he is not really being read; and if one feels oneself to be in instant and complete agreement with Bonhoeffer that may be because he is being misunderstood.

Reading Bonhoeffer has to contend with the very fact of his fame, the aura of heroism and martyrdom that encircles him and the reputation for theological radicalism that precedes him, all of which can encourage the reader to presume what he should be saying and to read into his words what he is *expected* to say. It is not surprising, therefore, that six decades and more of Bonhoeffer's posthumous existence in print have generated studies not only of Bonhoeffer himself but also of how he has been interpreted (and many, of course, would argue *mis*interpreted) at different times and in different contexts. It is therefore important that anyone coming relatively fresh to Bonhoeffer should be aware that he or she is joining a continuing and ever-moving stream of interest and study, and should have some awareness of the previous twists and turns of that flow and where it might be heading in the immediate future. We need therefore to sketch the story of the 'reception' of Bonhoeffer since his death, especially in the English-speaking world.

From a garden hiding-place to worldwide fame

At the time of his death Bonhoeffer's name was hardly known beyond his family, the small circle of his surviving students, certain colleagues in the Confessing Church and friends in the ecumenical movement abroad. Even within the Confessing Church he was regarded as a relatively junior figure (compared with such lions as Martin Niemöller), who after the closure of the Finkenwalde seminary seemed to have gone to ground in rather strange quasi-political involvements. From the beginning it was largely to Eberhard Bethge that the preservation and communication of Bonhoeffer's legacy were owed. Bethge, himself arrested in the autumn of 1944 when the full weight of Gestapo suspicion fell on the Bonhoeffer family circle, had buried much of the prison correspondence in a garden in Berlin for safe keeping. After the war he began to circulate copies of some of the letters to other former students and associates such as Albrecht Schönherr and Helmut Gollwitzer – both of whom in different ways were to play major roles in the post-war German Church. But the first edition of the prison correspondence did not appear in Germany until 1951, *Ethics* (which Bonhoeffer himself had always envisaged as his major work) having already been published in 1949.

Interest in Bonhoeffer began to generate in Britain at least as quickly as in Germany. In fact the news of Bonhoeffer's execution, and that of other family members, reached London from Geneva at the end of May 1945 while Bonhoeffer's parents were still awaiting word amid the chaos of Berlin. Very quickly George Bell wrote a short piece on Bonhoeffer, his life and the significance of his death, for the weekly *Christian News-Letter*, and arranged a memorial service for him and Klaus Bonhoeffer that took place in Holy Trinity Church, Holborn, on 27 July. The church was packed, and the service was broadcast by the BBC, including its overseas service. By chance it was heard by the Bonhoeffer family in Berlin, who thus received the confirmation of what they had been fearing. Bell continued to speak and write about his German friend as a witness to Christ and to that 'other Germany' whose cause he had advocated so diligently during the war. In fact there had always been great support in Britain for the Confessing Church – throughout the war services of intercession were held for the imprisoned Martin Niemöller, for example – and Bonhoeffer's death was seen as testimony to the ultimate cost that Christian witness could entail even in the modern world. It was not surprising, therefore, that when the first English edition of Bonhoeffer's 1937 book on discipleship appeared in 1948 it was given the enlarged title, *The Cost of Discipleship*. Bell wrote the foreword, quoting Bonhoeffer's declaration that the call of Jesus is his bidding to come and die, 'And this marvellous book is a commentary on that cost.' Thus was Bonhoeffer's image first shaped in the English-speaking world: a martyr who had not bowed the knee to the Anti-Christ.

The first English edition of the prison writings appeared in 1953 as *Letters and Papers from Prison* in the UK and *Prisoner for God* in the USA. In Germany there had certainly been interest aroused at their publication two years earlier. But German theology at that time was dominated by the controversy between Karl Barth and Rudolf Bultmann over the latter's proposal for 'demythologizing' the New Testament message in order to make it comprehensible to contemporary people. It was tempting for advocates of either protagonist to attempt to recruit Bonhoeffer to their cause, interpreting 'religionless Christianity' to mean either a furthering of Barth's early onslaught on 'religion', or as another version of Bultmann's demythologizing programme. Bonhoeffer had had positive and critical remarks to make of both theologians but that was because he was exploring lines of his own – for some time the significance of this was not fully recognized. In the UK, the first sign of serious interest in the prison writings in fact came just before the appearance of the English translation. In 1952 the veteran ecumenical leader and Christian social ethicist J. H. Oldham gave a series of lectures in London entitled, 'The Meaning of Christianity Today', published in 1953 as *Life is Commitment*. Oldham had known Bonhoeffer well in the ecumenical activities of the 1930s, and had even read *Act and Being* in the original German soon after its publication. He had now read the prison writings in German too and was impressed by Bonhoeffer's dual emphasis on the 'coming of age' of humankind and the biblical, Hebraic warning about speaking too easily of God. There was certainly an immediate flurry of interest in the prison writings in both the UK and the USA, as people realized that in Bonhoeffer they were dealing with not just a martyr but someone akin to a prophet as well. In the UK a major promoter of this new interest was the Scottish theologian Ronald Gregor Smith, who as editor of SCM Press, and with close personal ties to Germany, was taking a major part in the transmission to the English-speaking world of the newest currents of German theology and philosophy. His own slim, deftly written *The New Man* (1956) heavily utilized Bonhoeffer (as implied in its subtitle, *Christianity and Man's Coming of Age*), along with Bultmann and Paul Tillich. It was an eloquent argument for faith as both deriving from God's manifestation in history and leading into further human responsibility for history – not an escape from history – and proved seminal for a new generation of Christian social thinkers seeking a theological undergirding of their involvement in 'secular' society. A perceptive discussion of 'religionless Christianity' was provided in 1962 by the Welsh Congregationalist Daniel Jenkins in his *Beyond Religion*, which sought to develop further the notion of 'coming of age' in relation to the Pauline New Testament concept of maturity through faith in Christ. That same year, however, Alec Vidler, writing the concluding essay in *Soundings*, the volume of essays by liberal Cambridge theologians, could comment that while the importance of Bonhoeffer's prison writings had initially been recognized, 'they seem now in danger of being forgotten, perhaps because their contents are too disconcerting for Christians to live with'.[1]

Within months all that was to change, with the publication in March 1963 of *Honest to God*,[2] the best-selling paperback by John Robinson, at that time Bishop of Woolwich. Aided by a Sunday newspaper front-page article headlined, 'Our Image of God Must Go', the book was a public sensation. Robinson, whose scholarly reputation was largely in New Testament studies, had during a recent bout of illness read Bultmann, Paul Tillich and Bonhoeffer, and felt impelled to call for a re-examination of Christian belief, ethics and spirituality. The Church had long since ceased preaching a God 'up there', but was still implicitly teaching a God 'out there'. Bultmann dealt with the last vestiges of the former; Bonhoeffer had recognized that people had 'come of age' and no longer needed the God 'out there'; and Tillich supplied the new image of God as 'depth' or 'ground of being'. Whatever its use or misuse of Bonhoeffer and these other theologians, the book unleashed a new wave of interest in 'radical theology' and especially Bonhoeffer. Cynics asked what was especially new here, given that Gregor Smith and others had previously drawn on Bonhoeffer at least as perceptively, and also questioned whether it was still the case (in the UK at any rate) that no one took any real notice of anything unless or until it was blessed by a bishop. There may have been an element of truth here, but other social factors were now at work. The early 1960s effectively saw the start of the breakdown of that social and cultural consensus that had held sway since the end of the Second World War, which had seen Western (or at any rate British) society as founded on traditional Christian values, within which the churches had a recognized and respected role even if actual public participation in 'organized religion' was declining. With the 1960s came a newer, more self-consciously secular mood. Previously, organized religion had widely been seen to be 'a good thing' (even if one did not personally subscribe to it) because it was the 'mainstay of morality and values'. Now, however, those values were themselves either being seen as independent of religion or, more radically, questionable as values. The *secularization* of society now dominated the churches' agenda of concern. Bonhoeffer's diagnosis and his suggested remedies, however provisional, inevitably became caught up in the debates.

Those debates for a time were liveliest in the USA. In 1963, the same year as the publication of *Honest to God*, Paul van Buren's *The Secular Meaning of the Gospel* attempted to interpret the New Testament faith in largely empiricist terms (for example, belief in the resurrection means that the first disciples 'caught' the contagion of Jesus' 'life for others'). Harvey Cox's *The Secular City* (1965) celebrated secularity as closely faithful to the biblical paradigm of the distinction between God and the world. But a quantum leap in radicality was provided by the 'death of God' theologians. For William Hamilton, the 'death of God' evidently meant the radically provisional, tentative nature imposed on theology in the present. Thomas Altizer, on the other hand, actually meant that since the incarnation, God is no longer there in any transcendent form, but only as love. Bonhoeffer tended to be used by all such 'secular theologians' in a somewhat one-sided way, selecting his statement that we have to live 'without God' but ignoring the other side of the paradox, 'before God and with God'. It was as if Bonhoeffer simply regarded the Enlightenment as the gospel, instead of recognizing the Enlightenment as redefining the person who is claimed by the gospel.

Perhaps it was in reaction to this one-sided interpretation that, within the English-speaking world, it was the USA that now saw the most concentrated and long-lasting scholarship devoted to the whole range of Bonhoeffer's works now appearing in English, including the early *Sanctorum Communio* and *Act and Being*, as well as *Ethics*. In fact the first full-length study of Bonhoeffer in English, *The Theology of Dietrich Bonhoeffer* (1960), had been by an American, John Godsey.[3] But Godsey had written this as a doctorate under Karl Barth, who felt puzzled and hurt by some of the criticisms Bonhoeffer had levelled at him in the prison writings ('a particular thorn' Barth called them) and would not countenance their being included in the study. This for a time could only encourage the view that the prison theology lay apart from Bonhoeffer's earlier work, either as a fall from grace (if you were a 'conservative') or the grand finale (if you were a 'liberal'). Bonhoeffer scholarship during the 1970s and 1980s revealed a much more complex story of continuities in theological and philosophical categories that, as this study has sought to show, discourages any simplistic playing off of 'earlier' and 'later' against each other.

The single most important contribution to an understanding of 'the whole Bonhoeffer' was Eberhard Bethge's monumental and definitive biography, which appeared in Germany in 1967 and in English, slightly abridged, in 1970 (a full and revised English edition was produced in 2000). This not only tied Bonhoeffer's theological development into his changing life-contexts but, in particular, for the first time fully exposed the nature of his involvement in the conspiracy against Hitler and the extent of the ethical challenges this posed. Gone forever was the individual, saintly figure who had preserved his innocence, and in his place was the one whose martyrdom had involved becoming guilty for the sake of others. Here was not just a hero of the Confessing Church, but one whose relationship with even that church was by the end one of mutual scepticism, whose significant community was no longer a worshipping congregation but the circle of his family, conspirators and fellow-prisoners 'standing in' for their nation under judgement. What does it mean to love God and neighbour now? From now on, what does it mean to be church? No questions posed by Bonhoeffer are sharper, or more persistent, than these.

Ecumenical witness

'The Church is Church only when it exists for others.' Bonhoeffer's challenge has particularly been felt within the ecumenical movement, to which in life he put searching questions on the issues of peace and on the universal significance of the Church Struggle in Germany. The first general secretary of the World Council of Churches (WCC), W. A. Visser't Hooft, had been a faithful friend of Bonhoeffer during the war years and never lost sight of the importance of his witness for the post-war churches and ecumenical organizations, especially as their agendas moved to embrace the concerns of churches in 'the third world'. A major programme of the WCC in the 1960s was 'The Missionary Structure of the Congregation' that drew heavily on the Bon-hoefferian concept of 'the Church for others' and emphasized the orientation of mission not to the Church, but to the world.

It was, however, especially on the issue of *racism* that Bonhoeffer's witness was to be crucial, and above all in South Africa. There, under the imposition of apartheid, it was recalled that the German Church Struggle had been about the imposition of the so-called Aryan clause on the church. This, Bonhoeffer had declared, brought about a *status confessionis*, that is, a situation where the gospel itself was being displaced by an alien creed that must be resisted. Apartheid was similarly a heresy to be resisted, the more so as it was given religious sanction by a pseudo-biblical theology of white racial supremacy. Bonhoeffer was consciously drawn upon for inspiration by much of the church opposition to apartheid, for example by Beyers Naudé, who founded the Christian Institute in 1963 as a 'confessing' organization, and 'the Church Struggle in South Africa' gained currency as a description of the situation.[4] In 1982 the World Alliance of Reformed Churches formally declared apartheid to constitute a *status confessionis* and suspended the Dutch Reformed Church from its membership until after the end of apartheid. What proved even more controversial than such debates, however, was the WCC's Programme to Combat Racism set up in 1969, and above all its Special Fund, which from 1970 began to distribute financial aid to, among other groups, the humanitarian wings of political liberation organizations in Southern Africa. There was fierce reaction in some quarters, especially in Europe (and particularly West Germany), where the WCC was accused of 'supporting terrorism' despite all the evidence that funds were going only to educational, medical and social projects. Dietrich Bonhoeffer's name frequently came up in the heated debates. African church representatives, particularly, were not slow to ask why European Christians were so proud of their hero Bonhoeffer who had involved himself in conspiracy, but shrank from solidarity with Africans engaged in their own resistance to tyranny.

Bonhoeffer's call for ecumenical witness to peace has also been influential. The Reformed churches of West Germany in the 1980s declared nuclear weaponry to constitute a new *status confessionis*. At its 6th Assembly at Vancouver in 1983, the WCC resolved upon a process of mutual commitment to 'Justice, Peace and the Integrity of Creation' (JPIC), in view of the unprecedented threats posed by the arms race and systems of injustice: 'The churches today are called to *confess anew their faith* and to repent for the times when Christians have remained silent in the face of injustice or threats to peace.' As a programme JPIC, linking the concerns of peace, social and economic justice and the environment, reached its high point in the World Convocation on JPIC in Seoul, Korea, in 1991. But it has remained conceptually powerful for global ecumenism, and it is no accident that its most effective European impulse was generated by the churches of both parts of a divided Germany, which in 1986 at the 9th Assembly of the Conference of European Churches called for a specifically European Assembly as part of the JPIC process. Their proposal was made in deliberate recollection of Bonhoeffer's call at the 1934 Fanø ecumenical conference (see pp. 14–15) for a truly ecumenical council to declare against war, and bore fruit in the First European Ecumenical Assembly held in Basel in 1989, on the theme of 'Peace with Justice' – prophetically, just as the walls of Cold War Europe were about to fall. No less challenging has been the identification of the injustice of the global economic system as a *status confessionis* (notably by the German theologian Ulrich Duchrow, who consciously draws upon Bonhoeffer for his theological analysis),[5] which is being followed through as a major priority – a '*process* of confession' – through the World Alliance of Reformed Churches' programme, 'Break the Chains of Injustice'. Bonhoeffer is therefore continuing to provoke churches and ecumenical Christianity on whether they can settle for the traditional, analytical way of 'doing ethics' or whether a much more radical demand is being made upon them by the crises of the day, crises in which the gospel itself is at stake.

Bonhoeffer and contemporary theology

The contemporary theological scene is one that in many respects Bonhoeffer would hardly recognize, and one where his own presuppositions and approaches are not universally recognized either. Liberation theology, which from its main Latin American base in the 1970s made such a challenging worldwide impact, owed its genesis to its own reading of the Bible in the context of poverty and oppression, aided by Marxian social analysis and the educative process of 'conscientization'. From such a perspective Bonhoeffer's examination of 'religionlessness' can seem like a parochial, Western intellectualist concern when the real problem for the mass of the world's population is the lack of humanity (or, simply, bread). Bonhoeffer, who came from a privileged background, remained largely traditionalist in his social attitudes. Even so, a number of liberation theologians pay tribute to what they owe to Bonhoeffer for his clear recognition that the gospel relates to the whole of life, for his own discovery of the 'view from below' that involvement in the resistance had brought him, and his example of costly political involvement. Feminist theology has more difficulties with Bonhoeffer, whose writings often seem to typify white patriarchalism in a typically Germanic form – for example, in her correspondence with him in prison Maria von Wedemeyer, his fiancée, has to battle hard to get him to take seriously her own theological questions (*LL* 163–5). Only with the greatest distortion of the plain meaning of his writings (in *Ethics*, for example, on marriage as a 'divine mandate') can Bonhoeffer be turned into some kind of proto-feminist, and even some of the most revered elements elsewhere in his theology come under feminist critique. In her imaginary letter to Bonhoeffer the Korean theologian Chung Hyun Kyung reacts ironically to his depiction of Jesus as 'the man for others' whose example we are to follow: 'I appreciate your confession of the core of costly discipleship that is, being a man for others. Especially a man like you: white

European, upperclass, elite man.'[6] But she then asks how does '*Women* for others' sound, especially in the Asian context, and continues:

> 'Women for others' doesn't give me any new theological imperative or inspiration. Why? Because that is what we women have been for the last five thousand years of patriarchal history. Remember our mothers', grandmothers', and great-grandmothers' lives? They sacrificed their life for others: their husbands, their children, their communities.

Nevertheless, a number of feminist theologians do see in Bonhoeffer's treatment of human sociality, community and the createdness of bodily life important resources for a theology of human existence – not forgetting, either, that as regards his attitudes to women, Bonhoeffer the man is said by those who knew him to have been better than Bonhoeffer the theologian.[7]

Nor, without anachronism, can Bonhoeffer be directly turned into a 'green' or environmental theologian. Yet his emphatic 'this-worldliness' – fidelity to the earth – that runs throughout his theology, together with the stress he lays on the bodily and social nature of created humanity, are important resources for an ethic of the integrity of creation. The American theologian Larry Rasmussen sees in Bonhoeffer an inspiration for a Christian 'earth faith': 'Song of Songs, means, then, for Bonhoeffer and for us, living life to the fullest, embracing Earth and its distress as the way of embracing God and being embraced by God. It means both saving life and savouring life.'[8]

There is one area of theological concern today where Bonhoeffer seems obviously problematic: inter-religious dialogue. He at first seems to rule himself out of play here on two counts. First, his very Barthian Christocentricity would seem by itself to reject the validity, from his point of view, of taking non-Christian faiths seriously. Second, his later wholesale attack on 'religion' would seem also to dismiss all faiths except his own brand of 'non-religious' Christianity. This, however, is not the whole story with Bonhoeffer, with whom matters are rarely quite so simple. Certainly his Christocentric theology of revelation was honed to its sharpest in the German Church Struggle, codified above all in the Barmen Theological Declaration, with its stark affirmation that it is Jesus Christ alone who is the Word of God to be heard, trusted and obeyed. The prime target of Barmen, however, was *not* 'other religions' such as Islam, Buddhism, Hinduism, but the *pseudo-Christianity* of nationalism being promoted by the 'German Christians'. The issue was which God the German Evangelical Church believed in, and which form of Christianity it was committed to. Moreover, as we have noted (p. 15), there is the striking paradox that it was precisely at this time of his greatest 'Barthian' Christocentricity that Bonhoeffer was most disillusioned with 'Western Christianity', to the extent of planning to visit India and to learn from Gandhi about non-violent resistance and, indeed, of drawing on the insights of eastern spirituality. Bonhoeffer always drew a distinction between Jesus as the one to be followed and Christianity as a system of institutional life and practice. Christianity might have to learn from the non-Christian world what it means to be Christian!

As far as the prison theology is concerned, Bonhoeffer critiques 'religion' in general terms. He does not deal with 'other religions' by name, and certainly does not go in for disparaging them at the expense of Christianity. His main concern is to distinguish Christianity from its own traditional 'religious', other-worldly, individualistic and life-compartmentalizing form. Indeed, at one point he confesses to Eberhard Bethge that he wishes he could 'claim for Christ' some of the gods of ancient Greece about which he has been reading, and that he finds 'less offensive than some brands of Christianity' (*LPP* 21.06.44). It would certainly be a Christian misuse of Bonhoeffer for him to be put on display to impress people of other faiths on how attractive Christianity can be. The kind of inter-religious dialogue in which he could be most creative would be one in which different faiths explored how a religious tradition may be prophetically critiqued from within itself on whether it is fit for purpose to promote the divine peace and justice among people. We could then look for possible counterparts to Bonhoeffer in the other world faiths and explore what parallels, affinities and shared insights might emerge.

But it might well be argued that events have shown that Bonhoeffer got it wrong about the 'end of religion'. Religion today, it is pointed out, especially in its fundamentalist forms, is resurgent, partly in reaction to the very secularism that announced its demise. But at the heart of Bonhoeffer's critique of religion is the question of what it means to be *human*, and when he says that people 'as they are now' simply cannot be 'religious' he is not so much describing how things are as attacking those forms of 'religion' that are contradictory to humans being mature, responsible, living life in its wholeness. His critique does not in the end stand or fall by how 'popular' religion happens to be at any one moment. Indeed, his critique of religion as un-worldliness can equally be turned against fundamentalist religion as 'over-worldliness', an attempt to control the world in the name of God rather than living in the world in the way of God as shown in Jesus.

For the best part of half a century, the imminent demise of the 'Bonhoeffer industry' has been forecast. But it continues to thrive, with a steady stream of publications both scholarly and more popular. Why? In part it is due to the very nature of his work, which deals with fundamental questions of faith and ethics, the importance of which transcends time and place and will always invite new examination. In part it is due to each generation looking at theological and philosophical issues – such as the nature of the language of belief and its communication – in new ways and thus providing a fresh vantage point on Bonhoeffer (as on other theologians). In part it is because genuinely new discoveries continue to turn up, shedding fresh light on his historical circumstances and indeed at times his own biography. Also, quite simply, it is due to each new generation of students and other readers arriving on the scene and, having to reckon with the most traumatic events in Western history in the last century, finding that this figure who lived and died in the heart of that drama has to be assessed as well.

The continuing influence of Bonhoeffer is, in one respect, diffuse insofar as his theology impinges relevantly on already existing concerns and interests. Even Chung Hyun Kyung at her most critical finds nuggets of gold:

> What I like most about your theological imagination is your 'without God, before God, and with God.' Your words come alive more than ever in this time of so-called postmodernity. We cannot find a wholesome, orderly, powerful god anymore. It seems as if the whole world is worshipping in the sanctuary of a global free market in a religion of savage capitalism. Its ultimate god is Mammon. We keep asking where the good God is who once gave us so much security. When our god loses its definite character our enemy loses its definite character too.[9]

It is especially where the fundamental issues arise of what human life *is*, and how it is to be valued, that a theology such as Bonhoeffer's, which deals so centrally with the nature of human existence and with the centre of that existence as disclosed in Christ, comes into play most creatively. A recent example was an international colloquium in Berlin in 2009 on 'Hermeneutics of Human Life: Bonhoeffer and Bioscience in Dialogue' that explored the interpretative frameworks within which 'medical' decisions are made on such areas as in-vitro fertilization.[10] Findings about 'human nature' always involve interpretation, consciously or unconsciously, as Bonhoeffer saw in writing in *Ethics* about 'the natural' as part of the 'penultimate' sphere, and it is especially human life as *relational* that is crucial in theological understanding. Such explorations exemplify how theology can return to the public sphere instead of retreating ever further into a private religious hole, or attempting to dominate that public sphere in a way that denies human maturity and autonomy. It is the way of dialogue, which enables the Church 'to exist for others'. That is vital at a time when, thanks largely to religious fundamentalism, the role of faith in the public realm is increasingly contested as being destructive.

To say that Bonhoeffer's influence is 'diffuse' is not a negative comment but entirely positive. It is precisely by its being diffused in the atmosphere that oxygen is life-giving, and what Bonhoeffer has done is to give theology new life by opening doors and windows – not only previously shut but not even known to exist – onto the world, the Church, community, spirituality, human responsibility and not least the Bible itself. We should expect, then, to find that this figure who has both a wholeness and many-sidedness to both his thought and his life continues to be a stimulus across a wide range of interests and to exercise an unusually ecumenical influence. In the heyday of 1960s radicalism and secularity, Bonhoeffer was often regarded as the mascot of 'liberals'. Today one cannot presume on who turns out to be a 'Bonhoeffer scholar' or enthusiast. It might indeed be a renegade Lutheran who has long ago given up on the organized Church and is rewriting the creed. It might be a leading politician trying to maintain integrity in the pursuit of justice in public affairs. It might also be a high-church Anglican working out a contemporary theology of religious community. It could be a Roman Catholic nun from Central America exploring the prayers and poems of Bonhoeffer in relation to political struggle. Equally, it might be a Southern Baptist in Texas looking to escape from fundamentalism into a nonetheless biblically based ethic of social involvement. Or a nurse working with the terminally ill, for whom 'only the suffering God' makes sense. It might one day even be the reader of this book – or anyone asking the question with which we began, 'Who is Christ actually for us today?'

Notes

Introduction: meet the radical

1 Where an actual letter in *LPP* is cited, the reference given is the date of that letter. Otherwise it is the document number to be found in *LPP* (DBWE Vol. 8).

1 Bonhoeffer: a life in outline

1 K. Barth, *The Epistle to the Romans* (Oxford: OUP, 1933), p. 36.
2 The first English editions (London: SCM Press, 1948 and 1959) were given the title *The Cost of Discipleship*.
3 P. Best, *The Venlo Incident* (London: Hutchinson, 1950), p. 180.

2 Persistent themes: Christ, sociality, this-worldliness and 'one realm'

1 From translation in E. Robertson, *Christians Against Hitler* (London: SCM Press, 1962), p. 49f. A number of English versions of the Declaration are available on the internet.
2 On the possible affinity of this statement with contemporary 'green' theologies, see page 90.
3 Text used here is a translation by Edwin Robertson, 'Thy Kingdom Come on Earth: A Bonhoeffer Sermon of 1932', *Expository Times* 88 (February 1977). A new translation can be found in DBWE Vol. 12.
4 Robertson, 'Thy Kingdom Come'.
5 See e.g. Bonhoeffer's two Advent sermons preached in London in 1933 (*L* 337–47).
6 Bonhoeffer's German term is *Stellvertretung*, rendered in the earlier translations of *Ethics* as 'deputyship' and in the new translation as 'vicarious representative action'. This latter rendering undoubtedly spells out the fullest meaning intended by Bonhoeffer but, providing this is kept in view, there is still something to be said for the less cumbersome 'deputyship'.

3 The prison theology: 'religionless Christianity'

1 For a remarkable earlier statement on God as suffering, see e.g. Bonhoeffer's 1934 London sermon on Christianity and the handicapped, 'My strength is made perfect in weakness', based on 2 Corinthians 12.9 (*L* 401–4).

2 Space does not permit doing justice to the question that obviously arises here, on the role of the Holy Spirit in Bonhoeffer's theology. Bonhoeffer was definitely a Trinitarian theologian, who could write and preach powerfully on the Holy Spirit and for whom Pentecost ranked high in the Christian year (see e.g. his prison letter of 24 May 1944). Cf. Burton Nelson, chapter 3, 'The Holy Spirit and Christian Discipleship', in G. B. Kelly and F. B. Nelson, *The Cost of Moral Leadership: The Spirituality of Dietrich Bonhoeffer* (Grand Rapids: Eerdmans, 2003). It also has to be said that in the context of Nazi Germany, when there was much loose talk about 'the Spirit' (of nation, race, etc.), Bonhoeffer cautioned against speaking about 'the Spirit' without a firm Christocentric reference, that is, as the Spirit *of Christ*.

3 Stephen Plant argues that it was primarily in the circle of resistance figures that Bonhoeffer saw exemplified the 'world come of age'. See his *Bonhoeffer* (London: Continuum, 2004), chapter 8.

4 The English translation, *The World View of Physics*, appeared in 1952 (London: Routledge & Kegan Paul, trans. M. Grene).

5 A cogent argument for the influence of Dilthey's 'philosophy of life' on Bonhoeffer's prison theology is found in Ralf K. Wüstenberg, *A Theology of Life: Dietrich Bonhoeffer's Religionless Christianity* (Grand Rapids: Eerdmans, 1998, trans. D. Stott).

4 Bonhoeffer, the Jews and the Holocaust

1 J. R. Fischel and S. M. Orton (eds), *The Holocaust and Its Religious Impact* (Westport and London: Praeger, 2004).

2 See Rosemary Radford Ruether, *Faith and Fratricide: The Theological Roots of Anti-Semitism* (New York: Seabury, 1974).

3 London: SCM Press, 1974.

4 The theologies of Bonhoeffer and Greenberg are discussed in, for example, Larry Rasmussen, *Dietrich Bonhoeffer: His Significance for North Americans* (Minneapolis: Fortress Press, 1990).

5 From Bell's sermon at the memorial service in London, 27 July 1945, cited in K. Clements, *Bonhoeffer and Britain* (London: CTBI, 2006), p. 118.

5 Pursuing Bonhoeffer

1 A. R. Vidler (ed.), *Soundings: Essays Concerning Christian Understanding* (Cambridge: CUP, 1962), p. 244.

2 London: SCM Press, 1963.

3 London: SCM Press, 1960.

4 See e.g. J. de Gruchy, *Bonhoeffer and South Africa* (Grand Rapids: Eerdmans, 1984) and *The Church Struggle in South Africa* (Grand Rapids: Eerdmans, 1986).

5 U. Duchrow, *Global Economy: A Confessional Issue for the Churches?* (Geneva: WCC, 1987).

6 Chung Hyun Kyung, 'Dear Dietrich Bonhoeffer: A Letter', in J. de Gruchy (ed.), *Bonhoeffer for a New Day: Theology in a Time of Transition* (Grand Rapids: Eerdmans, 1997), pp. 14f.

7 See e.g. Ruth van Eyden, 'Dietrich Bonhoeffer's Understanding of Male and Female', in G. Carter et al. (eds), *Bonhoeffer's Ethics: Old Europe and New Frontiers* (Kampen: Kok Pharos, 1991).

8 L. Rasmussen, 'Bonhoeffer's Song of Songs and Christianities as Earth Faiths', in C. Gremmels and W. Huber (eds), *Religion im Erbe: Dietrich Bonhoeffer und die Zukunftsfähigkeit des Christentums* (Gütersloh: Chr. Kaiser, 2002), p. 187.

9 'Dear Dietrich Bonhoeffer: A Letter', p. 17.

10 Cf. J. Zimmermann, 'Third International Bonhoeffer Colloquium', *International Bonhoeffer Society Newsletter* 95 (Winter 2009).

A guide to further reading and other resources

The 'Bonhoeffer literature' is immense and ever increasing. What is offered here is only a guide for beginning basic but serious study.

Works of Dietrich Bonhoeffer

All the major works of Bonhoeffer have long been in print. The first English versions, however, were produced by a variety of translators over a lengthy period of time, not always using consistent rendering of the German and not always with the most reliable original available to them. This is now being remedied by the production of an entirely new series of English translations, based on the critical German edition of the 17-volume *Dietrich Bonhoeffer Werke* produced by Chr. Kaiser Verlag (now Gütersloher Verlagshaus) between 1986 and 1999. The English volumes ('DBWE') are being published by Fortress Press, Minneapolis, as listed below. Those asterisked have been referred to in this book:

Volume 1   *Sanctorum Communio: A Theological Study of the Sociology of the Church**

Volume 2   *Act and Being**

Volume 3   *Creation and Fall: A Theological Exposition of Genesis 1—3**

Volume 4   *Discipleship**

Volume 5   *Life Together* and *The Prayerbook of the Bible**

Volume 6   *Ethics**

Volume 7   *Fiction from Prison*

Volume 8   *Letters and Papers from Prison**
Volume 9   *The Young Bonhoeffer*
Volume 10   *Barcelona, Berlin, New York: 1928–1931**
Volume 11   *Ecumenical, Academic and Pastoral Work: 1931–1932*
Volume 12   *Berlin: 1932–1933* (this contains a new translation of Bonhoeffer's Christology lectures)
Volume 13   *London: 1933–1935**
Volume 14   *Theological Education at Finkenwalde: 1935–1937*
Volume 15   *Theological Education Underground: 1937–1940*
Volume 16   *Conspiracy and Imprisonment: 1940–1945*

A chief benefit of the series is that the texts are accompanied by helpful editorial essays and explanatory notes.

Works on Bonhoeffer

The essential reading is Eberhard Bethge's monumental biography, *Dietrich Bonhoeffer: A Biography*, revised edition (Minneapolis: Fortress Press, 2000). A worthy companion is Ferdinand Schlingensiepen, *Dietrich Bonhoeffer 1906–45* (London: Continuum, 2009).

A number of works have been referenced in the notes. An excellent recent overall introduction to Bonhoeffer's theology in English is Stephen Plant's *Bonhoeffer* (see Chapter 3, note 3). For a highly useful understanding of the prison theology, see Ralf K. Wüstenberg, *A Theology of Life: Dietrich Bonhoeffer's Religionless Christianity* (see Chapter 3, note 5), and likewise Jeffrey C. Pugh's *Religionless Christianity: Dietrich Bonhoeffer in Troubled Times* (London: T. & T. Clark, 2008). The *Cambridge Companion to Dietrich Bonhoeffer*, edited by John de Gruchy (Cambridge: CUP, 1999), offers scholarly but very accessible essays on the various aspects of Bonhoeffer's life and theology, and is unlikely to date quickly. For a detached and sometimes ironical survey of the 'reception' process of Bonhoeffer, see

Stephen R. Haynes, *The Bonhoeffer Phenomenon: Portraits of a Protestant Saint* (Minneapolis: Fortress Press, 2004).

Further information and other resources

The *Bonhoeffer Bibliography: Primary Sources and Secondary Literature* (Evanston: American Theological Library Association, 1992) is updated annually in the Newsletter of the International Bonhoeffer Society (English Language Section). The English-language bibliography is cumulated in the online Bonhoeffer Bibliography at Union Theological Seminary, New York: see <http://www.columbia.edu/cu/lweb/indiv/burke/archives/bonhoeffer/sources.html>.

The International Bonhoeffer Society (English Language Section) publishes a regular Newsletter detailing recent and forthcoming events on Bonhoeffer-related studies and discussions, new publications and so on. Every four years an International Bonhoeffer Congress is held, drawing together from all over the world specialist scholars and those with a general interest in Bonhoeffer. See the International Bonhoeffer Society website or email: <info@dbonhoeffer.org>.

On film, the best presentation on Bonhoeffer to date is Martin Doblmeier's documentary, *Bonhoeffer* (Journey Films, 2003), available on DVD (contact <www.journeyfilms.com>). It includes interviews with Eberhard Bethge, members of Bonhoeffer's family, his students, specialist historians and theologians. Discrimination needs to be exercised, however, over the repeated attempts to dramatize and fictionalize (at worst romanticize) the Bonhoeffer story whether on stage, screen or in print.

Index